PaPaw's POV
(point of view)

BY MIKE HARMON

★ ★ ★

PaPaw's POV by Mike Harmon
Photos provided by Mike Harmon
For ancillary rights information:
Mike Harmon: mikeharmon@yahoo.com

FIRST EDITION 2024

Cover & Book Design, Rae Ella House

———————

ISBN 979-8-89589-197-1
Printed and bound in the United States of America

TABLE OF CONTENTS

Table of Contents *continued*

PAPAW'S POV

THIS IS MY STORY.

*Hi, I'm Mike Harmon, a former Kentucky State Representative
and former Kentucky Auditor of Public Accounts,
and this book discusses how I tried to be a Christ-Center
Conservative in a fallen world as well as additional ramblings
from this Don Quixote Statesman.*

DEDICATION

This book is dedicated first to my Lord and Savior Jesus Christ
who made me a sinner saved by Grace,
just trying to get a little better every day.

Then to Mom & Dad who always taught me to do what was right,
and that hard work and determination eventually pays off.
Sadly, my father passed shortly after I filed to run for office the first time,
but I'd like to think he would be proud of me
just as he would be of my brothers.

Then to my wonderful wife Lynn (Peaches) who I love,
and who even if she wasn't always excited about me running,
stood by me and supported my efforts.

To my daughters, Tori and Lizzie, and my son-in-law, Mah,
I love all of you all dearly.

And finally, to my grandsons, Aiden & HaMoody,
who made me, PaPaw, and Lynn, Peaches.
Thank you for bringing so much joy into our lives.
The point of view (POV) of a PaPaw is something special.
May God bless both your paths.

PREFACE

I guess if you are writing a book about trying to be a Christ-Centered Conservative, it might be good to start with your testimony. To be honest with you, over my 25 years of running for office and my twenty-one years of serving, I started and stopped drafting this book with different, but similar titles.

I love the Lord with all my heart and all my soul and all my mind, but I wondered who was I to write a book with some of my earlier titles of "How to Be a Christ-Centered Conservative"? More than one person has called me a good man, but who is truly good but God.

That is why I thought I had settled on "Trying to Be…" as I know I am imperfect but that is the exact reason I need the love of Christ. That is the reason we all need Jesus. I'm just a sinner saved by Grace, trying to get a little better every day.

As you can see, at the last moment I switched the title to PaPaw's POV. The older I get, I realize I still put God first, but after God, my grandchildren have become such an important part of my life.

As to my testimony, I know some adults have had dramatic shifts in their lives going from drugs, alcohol, etc., and everyone sees the massive difference in their life. My story is a little different.

I don't recall a time in my life when I didn't speak with God. I was raised in a family that went to church every week. As I recall, I remember someone saying they had a drug problem growing up. Their parents drug them to church, drug them to Sunday School, drug them to Sunday night services, etc. We were not exactly that way, but we made every effort to make it to our local Baptist Church services each week unless we were traveling to visit with one of my grandparents.

MY FAITH

I'm just a sinner saved by God's Grace trying to get a little better every day. I do not recall a time I did not talk to God, but I made a public profession of faith while I was visiting my aunt and uncle's church near the Ashland, Kentucky area. At that Children's Church in Ashland, I accepted Jesus as my Savior, confessed my sins and asked for forgiveness.

It has been a continual journey since that day, and I continue to seek His guidance and His will in my life both personally and politically. I may not be a polished politician, but if you want someone who loves the Lord, loves his family, and who loves this country, and in that order, I hope you will think of me.

MIKE'S MISSION STATEMENT

"I HAVE NO DESIRE TO LEAVE A LEGACY,

EXCEPT,

THAT I SERVED MY LORD,

I SERVED MY FAMILY,

AND I SERVED MY COUNTRY,

WELL."

In this link below, I shared in this video while on the trail my story of seeking the Lord, facing challenges, and serving in the places where God opens the doors.

My Faith Story: Kentucky Mountain Bible College

https://fb.watch/ig0zMv4fas/ #Godisfaithful #christianity #college

Perhaps the time in my life that I struggled most (and told in this video), while running for State Representative the very first time, my Father passed suddenly and tragically just a few months after I filed to run.

I was able to make it to the hospital as I had a buddy at work that doubled as an EMT. He told me he happened to hear a call to my Dad's house, and he called up front to let me know something was going on. I phoned my Mom and Dad's house and Mom picked up and let me know that the ambulance was on its way. Dad was bleeding out from his rectum.

Thankfully, I was able to get to the hospital in time and was able to speak with my Father. Sadly though, they originally planned to give him O type blood while they waited for his blood to be typed but instead put him on one and then a second IV which we can only assume thinned what blood he had left too much.

By the time they typed his blood and got him on the elevator he went into cardiac arrest, and we heard Code Blue over the intercom. I hit my knees and prayed so very hard that God would spare my Father.

Although they did revive him for just a moment, the stress from lack of blood (they eventually pumped in 7 units, but it was too little and too late) caused him to once again to become nonresponsive and this time he did not make it back.

After his passing, they gave us a moment to see his body. I cannot describe the grief we felt at that moment. Since then, I have had people ask me if I was mad at God for not answering my prayers in the way I had hoped.

My response was always, no. But I was mad at myself for several years because I wondered if had I only had a little more faith, a little belief, would my Father still be here today? It took a while, but I did finally realize that His ways are not our ways and sometimes it is just not in God's will no matter how much we wanted it to be.

I also had concerns that perhaps my earthly Father was not in Heaven. He went to church for the most part except the last few years of his life. I knew he had accepted Christ and had been baptized as a young adult, but I just wasn't sure. However, God did comfort me and allowed me to know in a couple of dreams that my Dad had made it to Heaven.

Although I plan to stay in this world as long as God wants me here, I do look forward to the day when I am called home and first get to see my Heavenly Father and then get a chance to see my earthly Father. Oh, what a day that will be.

If you are reading this and you have any doubt about where you are headed when you leave this world, I encourage you first to read the Bible, God's Holy Word, and then also visit with a pastor you trust. I know it used to frustrate my youngest daughter when she would ask how I knew for certain I was going to Heaven. It may seem arrogant, but it's not intended to be. I just told her the truth. Jesus Christ is my Lord and Savior. He is the way.

And though I have more flaws than I care to mention, my salvation is secure because of my personal relationship with Christ. I have no doubt of my eternity. When she would ask again, but how? I had to repeat because I know, I have no doubt.

I recall when I was running for State Representative for the third time and it looked like I was going to win, somebody came up to me at a debate and said, "If you get elected, you are going to have to set your faith aside while you're in Frankfort."

I was very clear and said, "If I can set my faith aside, then really I have no faith at all." Before you say, "I've got to get cleaned up, get better, quit sinning as much, before I seek His forgiveness, His Grace, and His will," then I say you never will. The best time to go to Him is when you think you can't. You think you are not worthy? Well, I wasn't worthy, and yet He still gave His life for me. And guess what, He did the same for you. Before it's too late, please accept the best Christmas gift anyone has ever given you!

If I had one prayer (some might call it a wish) before I leave this world, it would be that my children, my grandchildren, and my son-in-law all know Christ as their personal Lord and Savior. I so desperately want them to know without a doubt that they will have forgiveness and eternal life and that someday, I will see them again in Heaven.

May God bless your life, your path, and your way.

Mike sitting at previous House Desk after name plate removed after becoming Auditor.

Great American
Brass Band Festival
(2003)
L-R Mike, Lizzie, Lynn

MIKE HARMON — 1998
State Representative Ad.
L-R Lynn, Mike,Lizzie, Tori

Mike Harmon State Rep Ad

CHAPTER ONE

IN THE BEGINNING

MISSION STATEMENT:

**I have no desire to leave a legacy,
EXCEPT,
That I served my Lord,
I served my Family,
And I served my country,
WELL.**

This was the Mission Statement I felt God gave me as I wandered the streets of Washington D.C. shortly after being elected to office the very first time. But first let's start at the beginning.

In 1996, I went down to vote, and I noticed there was only one person on the ballot for State Representative. I thought to myself that this is not Russia and people need to have a choice when they vote even if it was not me. So, I spoke to my lovely wife, Lynn (Peaches to our grandchildren,) and I said, "I'm going to pray about, but I think I should run for State Representative (of the 54th House District) in 1998."

So, I did pray about and in 1998, I told my wife I was planning to file. And she asked, "file for what?" I indicated State Representative. She had completely forgotten (or perhaps hoped I had.)

After this clarification she was like, "Well as long as you don't get hugging the ladies and kissing the babies confused, we should be good."

Since I was working probably 60+ hours a week at a factory, I asked her to pick up the paperwork. She went to the courthouse and picked up the information. However, when I checked, they had given her the wrong county information. So, I had to make sure I had the proper documents.

Great American Brass Band Festival (2004) L-R Mike, Lynn

Of course, my 1998 race would not be an easy one. In addition to working so many hours, I was a Republican in a heavy Democrat district. The district at that time was made up of two counties, Boyle and Washington, and both were only about 25% registered Republican.

My joke for Boyle County that actually remained accurate until 2018, was that the only Republican elected to a partisan political position county wide or lower was the coroner and that was just to declare the Republican party dead on arrival.

So, I did go and file and as it turned out, the gentleman who had been state representative for twenty-eight or so years decided not to run and there was a three-way primary on the Democrat side. The victor on that side was John Bowling, the Mayor of the largest city in the district, Danville.

Funny story: during their primary, John came to my door while I was dressed sloppily and doing some cleaning. When I answered the door, he put forth his hand and said, "Hi, I'm John Bowling and I'm running for state representative." I shook his hand and said, "Hi, I'm Mike Harmon and if you win the primary, I'll be your opponent in the fall." I think I caught him off guard, but he said, "It will be a fair and clean campaign."

He did win the primary, and we ran against each other in the fall. Like many of my races, I was more of a Don Quixote candidate charging at races that very few gave me hope of winning.

It didn't help that I was not a particularly good fundraiser. The very first fundraiser I had, I held at a local steak house. I had three people show up, my wife, my youngest daughter, and myself. I did at least raise $300.

Sadly, shortly after I filed to run for office, my Father passed away suddenly and tragically. It devastated all of us in the family. In some ways, me running for office was almost therapeutic for me as I would do hours and hours of door to door. Between the walking and visiting with people, it took my mind off my sadness.

Also, sadly during that time, a shooting at the factory I was working at led to the death of Patrolwoman Regina Woodward Nickles. I was working as an Assistant Manager of Manufacturing that night, when the Manager came in from outside and was telling me, "I can't get the blood off my hands."

Legislative Conference L-R Jane & Rep. Jimmy Higdon, Lizzie, Mike, Lynn

L-R Mike (PaPaw), Senator Rand Paul

When I asked what he was talking about he let me know that there was someone strange out in the field next to the factory and the police had been called. When the police investigated, unfortunately, the stranger, John Paul Works opened fire on the officers killing Patrolwoman Nickles. This occurred in October of 1998.

Why this is relevant to my race is in addition to me being at the factory that night, I also had an opportunity to visit with Officer Nickles' mother shortly thereafter. While doing door to door for the campaign, I ended up running into Nickles' mother and she invited me to come into her home. This was one of the most humbling times for me both as a candidate and a Christian.

She invited me in and showed me a card from John Paul Works' parents asking her to forgive them for what their son had done. Nickles' Mother looked at me and told me she did not hold them responsible for their son's action. She looked at me and said she was a Christian and even forgave their son and did not want him to receive the death penalty. However, she did want him to pay for his crime and be in prison for life for his actions.

I thought, I'm a Christian but would my faith be that strong? Could I find it in my heart to forgive someone who had senselessly killed one of my children? I just wasn't certain.

By the time the race was almost over, I had raised about $3,300. Given the lack of funds, I had to be very strategic with my funds. I purchased 250 one-sided signs that my wife and four-year-old daughter stapled together to make 125 two-sided signs. I also purchased several palm cards to leave at homes as I went door to door.

I had also tried to get creative and save money. At the factory I worked at, they would throw away tons of pallets that they were more than happy to let me have. I thought, if I could break these apart, I could make my own stakes and therefore would not have to purchase wooden stakes. Unfortunately, if you've ever tried to break apart a pallet, you would realize that they do not break apart easily. I spent about an hour and had only broken apart one slat for one stake. So, that didn't work out.

I did, however, devote what free time I had to knock on every door I could find, street by street until I walked almost every street in the district.

As it turned out, RPK (Republican Party of Kentucky) did polling in the area about three weeks out and to their amazement, I was actually competitive. They ended up spending about $7500 in direct mail pieces on my behalf but unfortunately, I fell short.

I received 43% of the vote. In the area, that definitely outperformed the numbers, but a loss is still a loss.

I prayed about it and decided to run again in 2000. That time I raised about $5500. I bought some more signs (this time double sided) and more palm cards and once again knocked on every door I could find and even registered some to vote.

Sadly, RPK did not do anything in this race and this time I lost with 49.3 % of the vote and by less than 200 votes. One member of the Republican Party of Kentucky at that time told me years later that he had laid awake at night for months after that wishing they had put just a little into my race.

That was also when I found out about the difference between a recanvas and a recount. I was asked since the race had been so close if I would like to do one or the other and they explained the differences, but the main difference was when they said a recanvas doesn't cost anything to me but I would have to pay if I asked for a recount.

Curious, I asked how much it would cost, and they said, "We can't tell you." I was like, "Can you give me a range?" They said, "We can't tell you." Given I had only raised $5500 for the race, and I didn't know if the cost would be $500, $5,000, or $50,000, as you can imagine, I said, "Well, I guess I'm doing a recanvas."

So, we did the recanvas, I lost one more vote, and I still lost the race.

After that defeat, I wondered if I should try one more time. I prayed about it, and I was like, "God are sure I should do this again. I'm getting pretty tired of losing." But after prayerful consideration, I decided to do i one more time.

Parade in Springfield, KY Truck Bed L-R Mike, Lizzie Cab
L-R Mike's Mom (MaMaw Janet), Lynn

This time the gentleman who had beaten me two times before decided not to run again. So, the Democrat Party ran a local attorney. As it turned out, that attorney had sued a lot of local doctors.

As you remember, the first time I raised about $3300 and the second time I raised about $5500. This time between fundraising and RPK help, I had about 35K. My opponent still had with the help of the Democrat party about 45K. However, this time God blessed me, and I won with 57.6 % of the vote and I became the first Republican to be elected to the state house from Boyle County in 102 years.

One key for me in addition to bathing everything in prayer was to every time I lost, I had to do a postmortem and try to improve on the things that didn't work and keep the things that did. Also, for me the most important thing was to knock on every door, and I mean every door. I know RPK (Republican Party of Kentucky) likes the apps and the analytics, but I'm old school.

There were also several interesting things that happened in that race. The first being that my opponent, Bill Erwin, and I debated twelve to thirteen times and on at least one occasion during a debate, my oldest daughter babysat for the Erwin's children.

The other item of note was an event held in Boyle County. For a while Boyle County would have what they called, "Rally in the Square," an event I think the newspaper either held or sponsored. It was somewhat like a mini–Fancy Farm but just at a local level.

During that event, a local Centre College student created a fictional character called Erwin Ocrates which was supposed to be a mash up of Bill Erwin and Socrates. The student created this character after seeing a debate I had at Danville High School in which Bill appeared to be suggesting that since he was a Centre Grad that he was far superior to myself. I even joked with my wife after that debate, that they were probably just surprised a poor boy from Junction City could string a few words together to make a sentence. I am not sure that was Bill's intention or even his heart, but it did seem to be presented that way.

So, this student, a supporter of mine presented his character by loudly spouting how intelligent he was and how superior he was during the pre-event. When the event started, the first person listed to speak was the famous Gatewood Galbraith. He bounced up to the mic and indicated the event had a flaw. There was no Pledge of Allegiance listed in the program, so he took it upon himself to go right into the Pledge.

Unfortunately, the speaker system was not very good so many didn't realize what was happening until he was well into the Pledge. In addition, the Centre College student, not hearing or realizing what was going on, continued to spout off until about halfway through the Pledge before he stopped and took a respectful position with his hand over his heart.

Two Democrats, one being the local Judge Executive, pounced on what happened and wrote letters to the Editor of the local newspaper indicating how disrespectful they thought the young man was and how I, as the candidate he was supporting, should have called him down and stopped him immediately.

This became a crucial moment in my race. I responded back with a letter to the Editor of my own. I started with a quote, "I have not had sexual relations with that woman," a quote I attributed to both President Bill Clinton and then Governor Paul Patton. I went on to explain how Democrats tend to lie, and I explained in detail the events how they actually unfolded. Needless to say, the sitting Judge Executive who was also up for reelection became concerned when many turned on him after I rebutted his accusations. He even went as far as to greatly increase his radio commercials. He did in fact win, but as indicated so did I.

After I won that first race, a KY state senator reached out to me and offered me a scholarship to Washington, D.C. for a conference of legislators know as ALEC (AMERICAN LEGISLATIVE EXCHANGE COUNCIL.) This was the first time I had ever been to D.C. As I wandered the streets of D.C. on a rainy day before the conference began, I felt as if God gave me my mission statement that I carry with me to this day.

OH, THE WORDS WE SHOULDN'T SAY.

After that first victory, I was at an event of the Youth Livestock Sale in Boyle County and I ran into an old friend and a bit of a mentor. I even had dated his daughter briefly. He was a well-known retired ag extension agent and loved by many, including myself. However, he was of the opposite political party.

When I saw him, I told him it had been rumored that he had given consideration to running in this last race I won. He indicated that was true but had changed his mind at the last minute.

Then I made a big mistake. I told him I was glad he had chosen not to run as he would have been a formidable opponent (and he would have been.) Well, after that conversation, he chose to run against me not once, not twice, but three times.

I was able to beat him each time. The first time by a large margin. The second time, in 2006, when everyone was down on President Bush and Governor Ernie Fletcher, I won by only sixty-two votes that night (sixty-three after the recanvas.) The third time I won by a large margin again.

So, the moral of the story is never, ever, tell someone they would make a formidable opponent unless you want to run against many times.

Great American Brass Band Festival (2017)
L-R Mike (PaPaw), Mitch McConnell, Elaine Chao, Lynn (Peaches)

CHAPTER TWO

THE STRANGEST THING HAPPENED TO ME ON THE WAY TO A STATEWIDE RACE

Around 2010, I felt as if God was tugging at my heart to make a run for a statewide office, but I wasn't sure how to proceed or which office to run for. So, I did what made sense. I spoke to people who might be able to mentor me.

I went and spoke with Senator McConnell at his Louisville Office. (As a side note I found it funny that his office was located so close to the Courier-Journal.) He gave me a couple of pointers and told me I should go to as many Lincoln Day Dinners as I possibly could in order to get to know people.

I followed that good advice, but it still didn't make it clear what would be a good statewide office to run for in 2011. So, I wrote down three of the six (technically seven since governor/lt. governor ran as a slate) and I prayed about it. And I prayed about. And I prayed about until I got so tired of praying, I said, "God, I feel like you want me to run statewide, but Your direction is clear as mud. If you want me to run, please make it a whole lot clearer."

About 2 weeks after that prayer, I got a call out of the blue from someone named David. David said a businessman out of Louisville was considering a run for governor and wanted to speak with me about the possibility of being his lt. governor running mate.

I had my answer and God had made it very clear. The funny thing was lt. governor was not one of the three offices I had written down. I tell people if you want to make God laugh, tell your plans.

That 2011 race taught me a lot and I made quite a few friends. However, it may have been one of the more challenging races I had over the years. Phil and I faced in the primary the sitting Republican Senate President and his lt. governor candidate, an immensely popular former UK Basketball player and now Agricultural Commissioner. There was also a third slate of the Jefferson County Clerk and her running mate.

Needless to say, Phil and I were not the favored sons in this race even though I was a sitting state representative. The machine was strong against us. At many events, the President or the Commissioner might be the keynote speaker and be given twenty to twenty-five minutes to speak while Phil and I might get thirty seconds to a minute if we were lucky.

I even remember when we were at the Jefferson County Republican Party Lincoln Day Dinner, Phil had spent a $1,000 to sponsor a table which was to receive a banner and get recognition at the event. I believe President Williams might have been keynote speaker and we were given zero time to speak. When it came to recognizing the $1,000 sponsors, everyone but us was recognized.

When they recognized elected officials, they acknowledged everyone individually except me which they did not recognize. Thankfully, a few of my colleagues yelled up front and they did finally recognize me. Poor Phil indicated never again would he spend a $1,000 on a table.

It was a tough lesson to learn. I also realized at least at that time, the smaller rural areas, although not always, seemed to be fairer when it came to recognizing us and giving us time to speak.

As it turned out, Phil and I came remarkably close to winning that primary with just about $145,000 and I believe to this day, had the third slate not been in, we probably would have won. President Williams was (and is) brilliant but his negatives were high.

Oddly enough, several months later after the General Election for that year I ran into one of Governor Steve Beshear's staffers and he indicated the night of my and Phil's primary, they were sweating bullets as they had polling data that Phil and I would have probably won in the fall had we cleared the primary.

However, God had other plans and that was ok. I had learned a great deal about running a statewide race and I had made a great many friends who would become especially important in my future pursuits.

CHAPTER THREE

BACK TO GRIND/
HARMON V. HARMON

After losing the 2011 primary for governor/lt. governor, I took a little time to pray and seek guidance. Of course, before the next opportunity to run statewide again, I had a reelection campaign for State Representative in 2012 and it was an interesting race.

The local Democrat Jailer Barry Harmon (no direct relationship that we found but maybe very distant) decided to run against me in the general election and so we had a race the press labeled as Harmon v. Harmon. Although it got pretty intense, we were cordial to each other, and Barry and I became good friends later in life. He even switched to being a Republican a few years ago.

But as for this race, it did solidify what I have always said. If you go and run your race and you and your surrogates do not go negative, then neither would I. However, if you go negative, all bets are off.

As it turned out, they did go negative, so I looked for something simple. My selection was nothing personal, just something related to the campaign. I noticed on his Facebook page he had himself listed as a moderate. Now that was surprising because I always thought Barry was at least somewhat conservative.

Barry had a Centre College student doing his Facebook page who must have not been able to handle helping a conservative. So, I took a screen grab and placed it on my website. Then I recorded a radio commercial something to the effect of:

"Hi, I'm Mike Harmon, your Kentucky State Representative. Apparently, my opponent says he's moderate and that's ok. But I'm a conservative, I've always been a conservative, and if you want to continue with conservative leadership, please vote for me, Mike Harmon."

Now after that happened, I saw Barry at a function, and he came up to me and thanked me because he had not realized that young man had listed him as a moderate. So, he had the young man change it to conservative. As you can imagine, this allowed me an additional opportunity and I took another screen grab and recorded another radio commercial.

"Hi, I'm Mike Harmon, your Kentucky State Representative. Apparently, my opponent now thinks he's conservative. He's just not sure what he is. However, let me assure you that I'm a conservative, I've always been a conservative, and if you want to continue conservative leadership, please vote for me, Mike Harmon."

And yes, I did win that 2012 election. I had another election for State Representative in 2014, but no one challenged me in that race. As it turned out, 2014 would be my last race for this office.

Over the years, I lost my first two races for State Representative and then won the next seven. Oddly enough, I never had a primary for this office and after losing the second race in 2000, I've never lost to a Democrat in any race since. Sadly, however, I've never won a Republican primary, either.

RUN STATEWIDE AGAIN?

And that brings me to my race for Auditor. After my 2011 loss, I felt like God was still tugging on my heart to run statewide again. I assumed it would be for Secretary of State since I had set on Elections, Constitutional Amendments, and Inter-Governmental Affairs for thirteen years.

However, every time I prayed about, God said no. My wife and I even took a couple of days and went to Potter's Ranch for a retreat and to pray. But the answer kept coming back, no.

So, I thought, that was it. I wasn't going to be running another statewide race even though I really thought God wanted me to run. But through a series of events and prayers, I felt led to run for Auditor of Public Accounts.

Now, I imagine every young child lays awake in bed at night thinking someday, "I'm going to be Auditor." No, but I did feel as if God wanted me to run for the office and so I did.

It was not an easy path. After it was found out I intended to run, Jesse Benton, a family member of the Paul's (Ron and Rand) reached out and offered to be my consultant for a small fee.

In many ways for the first part of the race, it became as much about Jesse as it was about me or the race. My opponent was the incumbent, Adam Edelen, who was immensely popular and who "rumor had it" was going to run a race against Rand Paul for the Congressional Senate seat in 2016 after he had dispensed with me in 2015.

Somewhere in the race, I received a call from Jesse indicating he had been indicted for violating campaign finance laws in a different race. That call occurred about ten minutes before I received an influx of calls from the press regarding the situation.

If you want to be prepared to handle tough situations like this, I suppose it was good training. And yes, I did let Jesse go and limped my way through the rest of the race.

I even remember this issue coming up in my KET debate with Adam and how he slammed me for poor judgment in having Jesse as a Campaign Manager. I had to correct him that he was a consultant and not my manager and that we had parted ways after I found out about the indictment.

I also countered that Adam had recovered from his poor decision of donating to Barack Obama as well as he had his own scandal in 2011 while serving in Governor Steve Beshear's administration. I explained if he could survive those two things and still go on to be elected Auditor in 2011, then my chances should still be good.

Both Adam and the moderator, Bill Goodman, appeared to be taken aback by the walk down memory lane of Adam's past and Bill chimed in that that was in past. I interjected that so was my issue and maybe we should move onto the next subject. We did quickly.

That debate also held a foreshadowing of things to come. After the lights went down and we were off air, Adam reached out to shake my hand and asked if I were to get elected, would I promise to continue his efforts to try and get the SAFE ACT (Sexual Assault Forensic Evidence) passed and I promised I would. In 2016, I worked with the sponsor, Denise Harper Angel, and she was able to get the bill passed.

I wish I could say things got better after the debate, but polling did not reflect. The very first poll that came out long before the debate did have me up by six points but every poll after had me losing by wide margins.

To make matters worse, my poor fundraising abilities had come back to haunt me as well. I had only raised about $45 Thousand compared to the $800 Thousand that Adam had raised. Also, people like Rachel Maddow were describing Adam as the next up and coming Southern Democrat comparing him to people like Bill Clinton.

And if the weight of that was not too much to bear, my oldest daughter married a young man from Syria who she met in Ghana, Africa. He was and is a wonderful young man and she eventually became pregnant with our first grandchild.

We ended up flying her back to the states when she was about 7 months pregnant and sadly it took us about 2 years and about $20,000 in order to finally get him out of Ghana and to the states. He ended up not being able to hold his first son for almost 2 years. I have included a link to an MSNBC article and video that was published shortly after my son-in-law finally made it.

MSNBC -
Reunion after almost 2 Years of Mah Tori Aiden

https://www.today.com/parents/immigration-ban-syrian-father-yearns-meet-american-son-t107665

I did find it interesting that they played up the immigration ban portion, but we had gone over a year and half under President Obama with no results. Shortly after President Trump got into office, we were finally able to resolve the issue.

In addition, had I not won Auditor, I'm not sure we would have had the money to help our daughter. I am so grateful to God and to the citizens of Kentucky for the opportunity to serve.

BUT WAIT, THERE'S MORE.

During this same time, while the election was going on, we also had a situation with our youngest daughter. She had been in a relationship with a young man who was very controlling, limited our time with her, and though we knew he was verbally abusive we were not aware of any physical abuse.

And although we tried several times to convince her to leave him, she would not. We even reached the point where we had to take away her key and change the locks for fear he might come in and do harm to our grandson.

The flashpoint occurred one night when I got a call in the middle of the night from my youngest daughter's phone, but when I answered the phone, it was her boyfriend. He was drunk and wanted to see my daughter. That was a surprise to me as I didn't realize she was already downstairs.

She had texted her sister who let her into the house after her and her abusive boyfriend had been fighting and he threatened her. What I found out that night was something new; in addition to being verbally abusive, he had also become physically abusive.

To make matters worse, he was holding her cat hostage and wanted her to come back to the apartment to get the cat. This brought on the remembrance of a friend of ours who had the same situation with her daughter and a pet dog. But when this young lady went back to get the dog, she was tied up and tortured for more than 2 hours before she was killed.

So, when I received the call from her boyfriend, I was still a little groggy from sleep, but I told him to go sleep it off (it was evident he was drunk) and we could talk about it in the morning. He instead came to the door and was banging on it relentlessly.

Now given I was a legislator and familiar with the Castle Doctrine, I knew if I needed to take action to defend myself or my family, I should be protected from prosecution. In addition, having just found out that night he had been physically abusive as well as memories of our tortured friend's daughter running through my mind, I would be lying if I said I didn't seriously consider resolving the issue in a way he would no longer be a threat to my family.

Thankfully, after a pause, cooler heads prevailed, and I called the police. I hollered through the door that I was calling the police. He said he couldn't believe I would do that through the door and indicated he should have gotten more violent. (I found out later that he had a drunk Marine buddy with him as well.)

When I called to report the incident the first question asked was "Do you have any weapons?" I said I did, but I had not retrieved them yet. I heard her say, "The weapons are secure." They did dispatch the police, and they did arrest this young man and put him in jail for one night for him to sober up.

I wish I could say that was that when it came to my youngest being with this man, but she did return to him, and we had a strained relationship until sometime later. I had to liberate her from his grasp and take her completely out of state to live with one of her friends. We even changed her phone number.

CHAPTER FOUR

WHEN MOMMAS PRAY GREAT THINGS HAPPEN!

But getting back to that 2015 race for Auditor, our youngest daughter, who, as I said, was dating a young man who had been abusive to her. We also found out during that race she had made plans to go to Colorado with this same boyfriend in order to start growing marijuana "legally." Now since my wife and I knew this was not a good thing at all and we were both concerned she might end up dead and buried in a field somewhere in Colorado, we both decided to pray. And pray we did!

Now you might ask, why isn't this section labeled "When Parents Pray?" I'm getting to that. My prayers were more like, "Lord, please protect my little girl and do not let anything happen to her." I found out later my wife's prayers were a bit more specific. Her prayer was more like this, "Lord, I know you are in control, and I know whatever your will is, it will happen. Lord, if my girl goes to Colorado, I'm not sure we will ever see her again. Please cause something to happen where she will not be able to have a way to get to Colorado, but please make sure no one gets too badly hurt, in Jesus' name I pray, Amen."

Matthew 21:22 says, "And all things, whatsoever ye shall ask in prayer, believing, ye shall receive." And John 14:14 says, "If ye shall ask any thing in my name, I will do it." Now I can tell you my loving bride had no doubt in her mind that Jesus could provide protection for our daughter and fulfill her request. Jesus is not a short-order cook or a genie, but he knows our heart and when we sincerely come to Him with our concerns, He listens.

After my wife's prayer and shortly before our daughter and her boyfriend were about to leave, an amazing but thankfully not tragic event occurred. There was an old man who made a navigational mistake and ran into my daughter's SUV. Thankfully, no one was too severely injured but the older SUV my daughter drove was totaled. Fortunately, the amount to be paid for the vehicle would not be enough to replace it. So, my daughter and her boyfriend could not depart on their adventure.

Thankfully, both our daughter and the older gentleman were able to walk away from the accident with minor injuries, but the event prevented our daughter from taking what may have been a life-ending trip. Needless to say, though both my wife and I pray, and we both believe in God's power and Grace, I will always take pointers from my loving bride on how to pray.

CHAPTER FIVE

YOU ONLY RAISED $45,000 FOR YOUR CAMPAIGN AND YOU HIRED A BARISTA?

After missing the possible deadly trip, I knew my daughter and her boyfriend would eventually find transportation and possibly make another attempt to go to Colorado, so I had to come up with a more permanent plan to prevent her departure or at least delay for months until I hoped she would come to her senses. After careful consideration, I did come up with a plan.

At the time my daughter worked as a barista at a locally owned coffee shop but didn't make a lot and I knew that job would not necessarily keep her in Danville. So, I decided I needed a driver to drive me on the campaign trail so I could stay on the phone trying to raise money and support.

After sitting down with her, I agreed to pay her $300 a week and she could also continue to work as a barista at the coffee shop but would need to keep the times I needed her to drive clear. I also placed a provision in the contract that if she stayed with me until the end and I won, I would pay her a $1,500 bonus.

Now she knew exactly what I was up to but agreed because she needed the money. And so, we began our campaign adventure. I love my daughter, but she is funny. If someone were in front of us, she could drive extremely fast, but if no one were in front of us she drove like a seasoned citizen.

During this time, I definitely enjoyed being on the road with my daughter and reconnecting with her. Unfortunately, at the same time, her abusive boyfriend was doing what every abusive boyfriend does and was working to poison her mind when it came to her family including myself. I think it really bothered him that he had not completely isolated her from us.

I can't remember exactly what happened but there was a time that I needed my daughter to drive, but her boyfriend wanted her to stay home and visit with him. I explained to my daughter that we were in the crunch time and I really needed her to drive.

Unfortunately, he did convince her to stay home. I had made it clear that if she didn't make it, I would have to let her go. But she went ahead and quit, much to my sadness. Later, when I won, she was happy for me but a bit sad she had not stayed as a driver because she forfeited her $1,500 bonus.

The funniest thing about the time my daughter was with me on the campaign was how I had reported her employment on my campaign report. I had always been my own campaign treasurer and did my own campaign reports.

As I understood how to report a payment to someone who worked for you but also worked somewhere else was that in addition to listing what they did for you, you had to list any other employment they had. So, in addition to listing her as a driver on my campaign, I also listed her employment at the coffee shop and her title as a barista.

I think it may have been Joe Gerth who was combing over my campaign report, what little there was of it, and asked me the question, "So you only raised $45 thousand for a statewide race, and you hired a barista for your campaign?!" Well, I guess if you don't have a lot of money for ads, maybe you have to stay caffeinated to cover more territory.

As I said, I truly enjoyed my time with my daughter on the trail. To be honest, in the 2015 race we faced so many trials and tribulations, it was nice to have something to laugh about. To this day, I know God was with me on that race because with all our challenges, there is no way I should have won that race.

CHAPTER SIX

STILL TAKE TIME TO LAUGH DURING TRIALS

While I served as a State Representative in Kentucky's General Assembly for thirteen years and as Auditor for eight years, we dealt with some pretty serious and heartbreaking issues. In order to maintain your sanity, I found humor to be a valuable tool, when appropriate, to ease some of the stress of these issues.

In addition, a corny or Dad joke (usually one I've appropriated from a pastor somewhere) is an effective way to get people engaged prior to a speech especially when your topic may not be as interesting to others outside your field as it is to you. When possible, a few jokes inserted along the way also help to bring people's attention back when you can see eyes glazing over.

I have a good friend (who also was my congressman) who says Mike always likes to start a speech with a good joke. And then he adds, "Well, Mike thinks it's a good one anyway."

One joke I told on the campaign trail and much to the chagrin of staff for some time after I was sworn in as Auditor, went a little like this: "There was this Kentucky girl who fell in love with an Indiana boy whose name was Clarence. She called her dad up and said, 'Daddy I've fallen in love with Clarence, and we are getting married.' The dad replied, 'Isn't Clarence from Indiana?' She replied, 'Yes, Daddy he is.' 'I don't want you to marry any Indiana boy. I hear they're mean and sometimes even throw a chair or two.' (That was a reference to Coach Bobby Knight.)

Well as you might imagine, the young lady had her dad wrapped around her little finger and she did go ahead and get married. About two years later the dad gets a call from his daughter and she says, 'Daddy, you were right, Clarence is being mean to me.' He said, 'Don't you worry, I'll grab your two big brothers, and we'll come up there and take care of old Clarence.'

So, they hop in the car, drive up to Louisville and cross the bridge into Indiana. Then right after crossing the bridge, the dad turns the car around and heads right back into Louisville. One of the brothers says, 'Daddy, Daddy, aren't we going to help, Sissy?' The dad replies, 'Boys, I'd love to, but didn't you see that sign when we crossed the bridge, Clarence, eleven foot seven.'"

You know, sometimes in life, we see giants. But we have to remember that God sees grasshoppers. There is nothing that if He makes it part of His plan that can't happen.

I told the Clarence joke during my race for Auditor because I knew I faced a giant in the money and name recognition of Adam Edelen, but I also knew if it were God's will, I could win. It's important to pray like it's up to God, and work like it's up to you.

Once I was elected Auditor and spoke to my staff, I also used the joke to relate that you must make sure you have the right information before you make a decision or report on an issue.

2018 Christmas Card L-R Lynn (Peaches), Mike (PaPaw)

CHAPTER SEVEN

ADAM, THANKS FOR THE HELP!

To say I had limited funds to advertise would definitely be an understatement. What little I had, I used for strategically placed radios ads, Facebook Ads, robocalls, palm cards and signs. But then something happened.

After Adam had run multiple positive commercials about what he had done in the Auditor's office, he decided to go in a different direction. I was at a Republican event somewhere when one of my supporters approached me and asked if I had seen that terrible commercial Adam ran against me. To be honest, I had not because I was on the road more than I was home.

When I finally did see it, I was surprised at the content. It looked as if Adam or someone on his team (Who has money for a team?) had reviewed travel vouchers for the last twelve to thirteen years of my service as State Representative and was trying to make it look like it all occurred in a year or two.

The commercial starts with on screen text of "Career Politician Mike Harmon" and a good picture of myself in the upper righthand corner. (This of course was funny that they used a good picture because trust me there were plenty of bad ones out there they could choose from.) In the background you see a plane hangar with a jet and embossed on the hangar floor was the same picture of me with the caption of "Air Harmon."

This video went on to say that I had billed the taxpayers over $20,000 traveling around the country to meet with special interest living the high life in places like Salt Lake City, Utah. It also had a body double shown from the back (He was a little heavier than me, but not that I fixated on that of course) boarding the plane and pushing the baggage handler in contempt.

But then they made a mistake. When the scene switched to inside the plane, they had my body double seated, and a pretty flight attendant served me what appeared to be an adult beverage. Now, I don't mind if someone else wants to have a drink or two if they do it responsibly, but I am a teetotaler and almost everyone knew that.

So, this commercial upset my Republican friends, but it also upset my Democrat friends. I had people at my church say things like, "When I saw commercials about Matt Bevin and Whitney Westerfield, I wondered if they were true. But I knew that commercial about you was a lie, so maybe the others were a lie too."

But the funniest thing was that even though most people knew it was a hit job, both my wife and I had multiple people come up to us and say things to the effect of, "Hey, I saw Mike's commercial the other day. It was really great!" Based on the number of times this hit piece seemed to run, it appeared to get more airtime than Adam's positive commercial about himself. So even though I couldn't afford to go on air with a tv commercial, Adam's efforts greatly raised my name recognition.

God turned something intended for evil into something good. I guess I should thank Adam, because I'm not sure I would have won if he hadn't attacked me. But once again, all things are possible if it is in God's will.

CHAPTER EIGHT

SO, YOU WANT ME TO DO WHAT, GOD?

To say the year 2015 when I first ran for Auditor of Public Accounts was a bit stressful would be an understatement for sure. Very little money, dealing with family issues on multiple fronts, still serving as State Representative, and trying to sell some insurance to pay bills (my regular job), were perhaps only a few items weighing on my mind.

I spent a great deal of time in prayer (and on the road) trying to fulfill the direction I thought God wanted me to go. And then something happened. Since I was definitely in a David versus Goliath situation, God laid on my heart to get five stones and place them in a bag that I would carry with me as a symbol of how He had delivered David and if it was in His will, he could deliver me as well.

You see, most people only remember the one stone that David used to slay Goliath, but he actually went out and gathered five smooth stones.

"1 Samuel 17:40 King James Version (KJV): And he took his staff in his hand, and chose him five smooth stones out of the brook, and put them in a shepherd's bag which he had, even in a scrip; and his sling was in his hand: and he drew near to the Philistine."

So, I began to look where I might find five stones. Now my wife had given me a gag gift a few years earlier. When I was young, there were three items I wanted for Christmas that I never received. One was a telescope. The second was a metal detector. And the third was a rock tumbler.

Now for those of you who are saying, "What's a rock tumbler?" Let me explain. It is a device that you put small nonsmoothed stones in with a sand-like substance and it tumbles for about a month creating a smoothed and polished stone.

This is a picture of the rock tumbler I took the 5 stones from for the 2015 Auditor race.

When I felt God tug on my heart to gather five stones, I pulled the rock tumbler off the shelf, dusted it off, and proceeded to gather five stones from the box. Now I would love to tell you the stones were smooth like David's. They were not.

My wife always says they could have been had I actually used her gift, but I had not. I took the five rough stones (maybe a good symbol of who I really was) and I placed them in a sandwich bag that I carried in my pocket. That was about three weeks from the election.

About two weeks before the election, I ran into a good friend of mine who I served with in the House. He was actually of the opposite party, but a man of strong faith who I had grown to appreciate as a friend. I showed him the stones and explained why I was carrying them.

He told me how great that was and said, "Wait, I have a book I want you to read." Now I hate to say it, but I am a slow reader. I usually absorb a lot but still I'm no speed reader. I told him I appreciated it, but I was getting up before everyone else and my head was the last to hit the pillow. It was the only way I felt as if I had any chance at all.

My friend just smiled and told me not to fear. He marked about eleven pages in the book and asked me to read just those pages. The book was David and Goliath by Malcolm Gladwell.

I did read the eleven pages. I forgot part of it, but the part that stood out was that the underdog wins one-third of the time. This was something I didn't realize. It went on to explain that you have to trust completely in the Lord and leave it all on the field. I also kind of added that you have to go just a little bit crazy.

The day of the election, I continued to bathe the election in prayer. In my conversations with God, I said I was tired of telling the same success story over and over again. For years, I would tell the story of how I had lost my first two races for State Representative before I won on the third try becoming the first Republican from Boyle County to win State Representative in 102 years.

It was a good, true story. But I was tired of hearing myself tell the story over and over, so I asked God to give me a new story. I also prayed a prayer of Jabez in asking for God to increase my territory.

The night of the election, my family and I headed to the hotel in Louisville where most statewide candidates were going to be, and we actually were five minutes from the hotel when we hit a bad traffic jam. That five minutes turned into an hour.

So, by the time we got to the hotel, the results were already coming in from the Eastern Time Zone. I had told my wife that if I could stay close in the Eastern Time Zone, I thought I had a chance to win.

As the results came in, the lead went back and forth between myself and Adam. I asked my friends and family to get together to pray. Phil Moffett who I had run with in 2011 was there as well as Stan Lee (not the comic book guy) who I had served with in the KY House.

I asked that we hold hands, and I prayed what I tell most people was a "Facing The Giants" type of prayer. "Facing The Giants" was a Christian movie that had come out a few years earlier. I say it was like because I started the same, "God I'm going to Praise you whether I win and I'm going to Praise you whether I lose." But then I added however, "but Lord, I could use a victory."

Amazingly at that moment, the totals flipped back in my favor, and it never flipped back. I won by four percentage points a race that the last poll had me listed as down nine. I was extremely thankful. It was a miracle I will never forget.

It wasn't too long after that someone reached out and asked, "Where are you?" Adam had conceded the race and I needed to get down to the ballroom to give a speech. Strangely enough I had not prepared a speech for either outcome.

But they hustled me downstairs and into the ballroom. As they were moving me through the crowd, I turned to someone and said, "Huh, dog catches car." They placed me onstage with my family, my friends and colleagues.

I simply spoke from the heart. Someone hollered out, "Clarence" and I responded, "Clarence, 11 foot 7," which was a reference to my Clarence joke. I went on to praise God and to thank the people. I explained that it's not always about the money, it's about the people.

I also told the story of the five stones and how God had led me to pick up five stones as a symbol of the "David and Goliath" race that I had. I went on to say, "I read the Book. And David won!"

It was a wonderful evening and one I will never forget as I became the first Republican in Kentucky to be elected Auditor since 1967.

Election Night 2015 Coverage Mike Harmon Speech
https://youtu.be/SDePfMZeryU?si=Y5DzCg1nThuH4Z4t

Governor Bevin Inauguration L-R Lynn (Peaches), Mike (PaPaw),
Jon Voight, Lizzie, Medal of Honor recipient Dakota Meyer

Governor Bevin Inauguration Parade
L-R Lynn (Peaches), Mike (PaPaw)

Governor Bevin Inauguration L-R Mike
(PaPaw), Mike's Mom (MaMaw Janet)

On the Trail during 2015 Auditor Race L-R 'The Banjo Man' Neal Jame, Mike (PaPaw)

That time Matt Bevin wanted a photo of me in front of a plane to tweet out
even though my opponent Adam had a hit ad as if I had one. 11022015

Governor Bevin Inauguration L-R Aiden, Tori

Governor Bevin Inauguration
L-R Aiden, Mike (PaPaw)

Mike filing to run for Auditor in 2015, January 23, 2015
L-R Mike (PaPaw), Reporter Jack Brammer, Mary Sue Helm

2015 KY Republican Constitutional Officer Slate
L-R Whitney Westerfiend, Steve Knipper, Allison Ball, Matt Bevin,
Jenean Hampton, Mike (PaPaw) Harmon, Ryan Quarles

CHAPTER NINE

THREE SONGS

During my campaign for Auditor in 2015, I traveled many many miles on the road. A great many of those miles I traveled alone. I developed somewhat of a routine I relied on when I got back on the road after a speech.

There were three songs that I always tried to listen to when I got back on the road after a speech during the 2015 race. The first was "Voice of Truth" by Casting Crowns. The second was "Walk On" by The Kentucky Linemen (friends I grew up with.) And the third was "You Dropped a Bomb on Me" by the Gap Band.

Each of these songs had a special meaning for me (as well as I used them to keep me awake.) The lyrics to the first two songs were very inspirational. "Voice of Truth" speaks to the faith to face giants and walk on water. People mocked but when we listen to the Voice of Truth (God), He can help us overcome any adversity. That doesn't mean we always get the outcome we want, but it does mean all things are possible with God's help.

"Walk On" had lyrics that were also inspirational in describing that you will never succeed unless you take the chance. I'm including some of the lyrics below.

Chorus
You can't run the race
If you're standin' still
You can't swim to the other side
If you don't jump in
You'll never reach first base
If you don't leave home
Life is like a stage with a role to play
But you gotta' walk on

Verse

No one said it would be easy

That first step is a tough one

The game of life can be risky

And you can bet you're gonna lose some

You can spend your whole life

Wishin' and a waitin'

When just down the road

Is a pot of gold

That's yours for the takin'

During the course of my race, I asked if I could use part of the song in a video history of myself and my friends agreed. The video was about 8 minutes, but the song was just used in the opening.

As for, "You Dropped a Bomb on Me," I had fond memories of one team of wrestlers (who I can't remember right now) who would strut into the arena with that song as a signal of defiance that no one was going to stop them. It was my hope that those songs would symbolize the eventual outcome of my race even though very few gave me a chance of victory.

Thankfully they continued to inspire me and to keep me awake and, in that race, God did bless me with a victory.

CHAPTER TEN

OH, THE CARS I WOULD LOSE!

During the course of my four statewide races, there seemed to develop a habit of losing at a minimum at least one car a race. But the average was much higher than that amount.

While engaged in my 2011 race on the slate for governor/lt. governor, the governor Candidate, Phil Moffett asked me to go to Pikeville and speak at Hillbilly Days on behalf of the slate. This is when what I call the Pikeville curse started.

Of course, this was no disrespect to Pikeville or Pike County as they are near and dear to me, but apparently my modes of transportation have not felt the same. It was this first event in 2011 when I was driving into Pikeville my car started making a noise and acting funny. I pulled over to check the tires, but all seemed fine.

I pulled back onto the road, but it was apparent something was going on as one side of the back tires seemed to wobble. I pulled into a car dealership, Walter's I believe, and asked if I could park my car there until I got back from Hillbilly Days, and they told me that was fine. I called some supporters to pick me up and take me to the event, I gave my speech, and they brought me back.

Once I got back, I asked if Walter's could take a quick look at my car to see if they could figure out what was wrong. The rear axle had broken and that's why I was having the trouble. I was a bit sad as I had hoped to get back in time to see my daughter's play.

So, I did what most determined dads might do and asked if they had some used cars I could look at in my price range. As it turned out, they (being a car lot) had many cars I could look at. However, the one I selected was a used Lexus that had literally just been traded in. So much so that they had not even had a chance to clean before letting me test drive.

I tried it out, called and spoke with my wife, and ended up buying it that day. The car dealership cleaned the vehicle up while I was doing the paperwork, and I was on the road fairly quickly. The car I traded in ended up locking up the rear wheels as they pulled around back.

On the way back home, I stopped to get gas since it didn't look like I had much. However, when I tried to open the gas cap, I couldn't get it to open. So, I had to drive back to the dealership, and they proceeded to have similar problems but did eventually get open with the assistance of a flathead screwdriver. As it turned out, I did make it home in time to see my younger daughter's play.

That was the first time I experienced the Pikeville Curse, and I wouldn't see it again until after my 2015 race for Auditor. But that didn't stop me from losing vehicles along the way in 2015. As a matter of fact, I drove four different vehicles during the 2015 race.

My first car I lost in my 2015 race was the same one that I had purchased in 2011 at the beginning of the Pikeville Curse. This was the old Lexus I spoke about previously. It had been a good car over the last 4 years, but sadly my decision to run statewide again and all the road travel involved with that task was more than the old girl could take.

Somewhere along the line, I believe at an event in Bardstown, my transmission started to let me know I might want to check into other options. I did seek out and found someone to take a look at, I think over in Stringtown in Mercer County. As I recall, the verdict was not good, so I sought and bought another used vehicle at Spirit in Harrodsburg (no longer there.)

That one was a van. As I recall it was a Chevy Uplander. It had a lot of space to carry stuff and people. I was so excited because I assumed it would be great for transporting signs (even though I still had my Father's 1997 Chevy S-10 PU, but it had aged significantly.)

And it was great! (For about a month and a half.) I was scheduled to speak with a group of CPAs in Lexington at as I recall the Campbell House, but I needed to turn left on an extremely busy road. There was a flashing yellow turn arrow as well as a green traffic light beside it indicating you can only go if the turning path is clear. After a couple of cycles, it did not appear it also had a turning green arrow.

So, I did what I always do in such cases. I eased into the lane while the arrow flashed yellow, and the other light was green. Now in past events, you could wait until the green light turned red and assume it was red on the other side and go ahead and turn before traffic started flowing the other way. But this was not the case on this day.

The light went red on my side, so I assumed the through traffic on the other side was red also and began my turn. Now I was too far into my turn before I realized pretty quickly that at least one individual was going on through whether I wanted him to or not. I gunned it in hopes of avoiding a collision but sadly I was not successful and the man coming through T-Boned me.

Now the man who hit me claimed the light was still green on his side and maybe it was, but I did wonder. Either way, we both pulled into the parking lot, called the police to come and complete an accident report and waited. They did come out, wrote up the report and then headed off.

But my task was not over. Even though I had been through an accident I still had a job to do. I was to give a speech and answer questions from a group of CPA's. Well, I would love to say I wasn't fazed by the accident.

But I was pretty shaken up. However, I went in there, composed myself and presented just as planned. I'm not sure if I did a fantastic job or poor one as I don't remember much, but I got it done and got out.

Thankfully my van was still drivable, so I headed on home and began the process to have the van fixed or at least I had hoped and expected to. But even though the only real damage was to the sliding side door, the insurance company totaled the vehicle since they said it was too expensive to rehang a new door. Who knew?

So, I proceeded onward to my third vehicle of the 2015 Campaign. I went back to Spirit in Harrodsburg and looked at a couple of vehicles before

I settled on a new 2015 Chevy Sonic. This was just a step up from the next cheapest vehicle the Chevy Spark. At that time, the Spark seemed like a little tin can, and I think I could have picked it up and put it in a bag if I couldn't find a parking spot.

Though it wasn't great for transporting signs, the Sonic was great on gas and as I recall prices were up at that time and as I traveled the state, I put a lot of miles on the vehicles. I really enjoyed this car, but it too fell victim to my auto woes, although not permanently like the van.

One night, about a month before the election, I was in Somerset to attend a Republican event when a vehicle in a hurry popped up over a hill on a raining night as I was trying to turn into the event. The other car, though applying brakes slammed right into the back of my auto doing significant damage to the car (and a little to me.)

He was apologetic and explained he was running late to his son's football practice. We both pulled off to the side but were still close to the road when someone else popped over and almost hit us both. We then decided maybe it would be best to go ahead and turn into the event parking more off the road. The gentleman that came over the hill and almost hit us (even though he too was going fast) proceeded to berate us even though we had pulled into the parking area.

The police did eventually get there and took down the report. After, I was able to head into the event even though I was a little shaken. As it turned out, one of my legislative friends who also was an attorney came over and handed me her card and offered to represent me.

I ended up going through the insurance process myself (though I probably should have had her represent me,) but that same individual did become a part of my administration after I won and served the state and my administration well. She played a significant role in my successful two terms as Auditor, and I will always be thankful for her efforts.

Even though I had gone through another accident, I did have just as before, a job to do. I went ahead and attended the event, gave my speech and networked with Republicans there.

As it turned out, that was about a month before the election and thankfully the insurance company of the individual who hit me provided a rental car for that last month of the election while my Sonic was being worked on. During that month, I put over 5,000 miles on the rental car.

Oddly enough, they were fine with that as they said it all balanced out. Shortly after I won, I did get my Chevy Sonic back and somehow it survived my adventures during the 2015 race. However, its luck would run out in the 2019 race for reelection.

TURN AROUND, DON'T DROWN

In 2019 while I was running for reelection for Auditor, the Pikeville Curse came back. I had attended a Republican Lincoln Day Dinner (as well as a fundraiser for Sen. Phillip Wheeler) in Pikeville and was heading back home on the Mountain Parkway when we, (I had a young man helping on the campaign as well as a friend who had bummed a ride in the vehicle as well) were diverted by the State Police off the Parkway to avoid a mudslide.

What they didn't tell me (I don't imagine they knew) was on the road they diverted us onto was beginning to have the water rise. Oddly enough, the young man, Evan, who was helping, was driving my car but going soooo slow that both myself and the other individual, David, thought it might be best for me to take over the driving so we could get home in a timelier manner.

As it turned out, shortly after I took over driving (and driving more quickly), we ran into water pooling up on the road. Since it was dark and not in an area that had streetlights, I didn't see it until we were right on it and by that time it was too late to stop. Now I might have been able to stop and back out, but we were so far in, I was afraid the car would stall out.

In addition, I could see the other side of the road not underwater was not too far away, so I assessed it would be safer to push through and come out on the other side and head on home. But I was wrong.

Unfortunately, the car did stall out and we did not make it to the other side. But since I could see the other side close, I decided to get out and push the car out. So, I took my shoes off since they were a nice pair, put the car in neutral and proceeded to the back to push. Now I had assumed one of the young pups would at least steer, but I turned around and they were both up on a hill. In hindsight they were probably the smarter ones, but I had no desire to be stuck 3-4 hours from home.

But before I could start to push, I noticed a truck on the other side of the road with its lights on. The truck eased into the water and just passed where I was by the car. The driver hollered out the window asking if I needed help getting my car out and I indicated I did. He said he had a chain but he needed me to keep my foot on the brake in his truck so it wouldn't stall out.

I walked over (still with just my wet socks on since I left my shoes in the car) and placed my foot on the brake while he went to try and attach the chain. But he couldn't find a good place to attach and was afraid he might damage my car. He offered to take me into town (Salyersville) to see if we could find a tow truck company to help.

Looking back, I'm not sure it was a wise decision to hop into a truck with a complete stranger, but desperate times required desperate measures. And yes, I hopped into the truck with a full suit, tie, and wet socks and all and we headed into town. As a side bar, I will note that due to a lack of space I did abandon my two passengers on the hill they had fled to, but I did have plans to return after gaining help (even though they fled and did not help steer earlier lol.)

We arrived in Salyersville, and he took me to Speedway where I asked for help and I began calling tow truck companies. However, if they weren't already tied up, they themselves could not get out as they were trapped by the flooding.

My next idea was to call my Chief of Staff Sara Beth. She answered the phone and asked if I wanted her to come get me. The answer of course was "no" as we didn't need anyone else trapped in the region. She suggested a gentleman from the area, but when I called, he said he would love to help but he was in Florida.

He did suggest I call a local legislator friend I knew in the area, Representative John Blanton. When I called, John indicated he would love to help, but he too was trapped in his house. He did put me in contact with a local gentleman, Ritt Mortimer, who in addition to running the local newspaper and tv station, also had a second story B&B we could crash in for the night.

I had the gentleman who picked me up in the truck take me back out to the site, but before we could turn off the Mountain Parkway to the sideroad, we discovered that was blocked also. I was able to speak to Law Enforcement about my friends and apparently, they had hiked up to a connector further down the Mountain Parkway.

One of the Sheriff deputies helped connect us and took the three of us to a local emergency shelter while we waited for Ritt to come pick us up. As you may recall, I was still dressed in a full suit, tie, wet socks and no shoes.

But as to not waste an opportunity, I started introducing myself to others in the shelter. "Hi, I'm Mike Harmon, KY State Auditor." One gentleman came over and said he wanted to introduce me to his wife. "Hi, I'm Mike Harmon, KY State Auditor."

"Mike Harmon," she said. "Mike Harmon. . . I know a Mike Harmon, but he's a mortician." Now it had been a pretty rough day and as I spoke to this lady, I was still dressed in a full suit, tie, wet socks, no shoes and yet I still was able to reply back, "Well, that's where we differ. Everyone's dying to see him, but nobody wants to see the Auditor."

Eventually, Ritt did show up and picked us up to take us to the B&B. As a funny note, Ritt was the reporter who covered the news story a few months earlier about the previous judge executive referring to me as "Hatchet Harmon." Apparently, the Judge was not excited about one of my audits of the county. Now we never got asked by the press, as I recall, but we were prepared if asked with something to the effect that was a previous Auditor (Ed Hatchett.)

Before Ritt took us to the B&B, he indicated he was going to take us to Speedway to get some food as he didn't have food at the B&B. When we got there, still dressed in a full suit, tie, wet socks, no shoes, I introduced myself to the young man behind the counter. "Hi, I'm Mike Harmon, KY State Auditor." He shook my hand and then we went to check out what was available at that time of night to eat.

I then hear the young man behind the counter get on the phone. "Hey. . . guess what? We've got the KY State Auditor here. . . and he's not wearing any shoes. . ." We proceeded to take our selection to the counter. The cashier must have felt bad for me as he gave me a discount on the purchase.

After paying for our items and hopping back into the car, Ritt took us to his office as the B&B was on the second floor. I'm not sure how much comfort it was heading to the B&B when we drove through rising water by the B&B, but he said it would be fine and it was on the 2nd floor.

As we entered the building, Ritt pointed out a bottle of bourbon and told us to feel free to get a drink. I thanked him, but indicated I was a teetotaler. David quickly quipped tonight would be as good a time as any to start, but if I wasn't he would be happy to take my portion as well.

We eventually settled in. I took off my wet socks (still no shoes since they remained in the car), my tie, and my suit and went to bed. Sleep did not come easy, but we did get some rest.

In the morning, Representative Blanton came and picked us up. Imagine his surprise when he came to the door, and I had dressed once again in my full suit and tie. However, this time there were no wet socks (they were still drying) and I was instead in my bare feet.

He was surprised, but we all hopped in his car and went to McDonald's via the drive through, got some food, and waited for the Dollar General Store to open. Once the Dollar General Store opened, I went in with no objection to the fact I was barefoot, bought some socks and a pair of tennis shoes that oddly enough was a surprisingly good match for my suit.

We then proceeded back out to the spot where I left my car to see if it was even still there or if it had been swept away. The car was still there in basically the same spot, but unfortunately, the water had risen up into the car and probably got as high as the dashboard.

This was important to note as although I had taken my dress shoes off the night before to try and preserve them, unfortunately I did not place them on the dashboard but on the car floor. So, my car was totaled, my shoes were ruined, and I had lost $1,000 of campaign materials that I had picked up shortly before that was in my trunk. But thankfully no lives were lost.

Another strange oddity was that I had just signed up for monthly internet in my car the very day that the car ended up being lost in the flood. Though I paid for a month, no refund was forthcoming even though I only enjoyed it for a day.

In addition, Ritt had asked John to interview me in front of my car, so here I stood with my suit from the night before on in my new socks and new tennis shoes. Later, when this story spread and my home newspaper also interviewed me about it, some readers would place in the comments, "TURN AROUND, DON'T DROWN." I even have people tell me, "You know, that's how former Governor Burt T. Combs passed away.

I can assure you if I could have avoided it, I most definitely would have. I was, however, able to turn the event into a funny story that I not only told at events but was asked to tell at many others. I ended up calling a tow truck to haul my car off locally and called my insurance agent to take care of it.

However, that did leave me with the problem of being stuck 3-4 hours from home with no car. Representative Blanton was truly kind however and lent me his car since he was going to be back in Frankfort that week and could pick it up then. He was very trusting considering my history with cars.

Even though it was sunny that day, many of the main roads were still covered by water and it took us a couple of times to find the correct route out of Magoffin County. And no, I did not try to go through water that day when I could actually see the road.

We got home that evening, and I dropped Evan and David off. Strangely, David never tried to bum a ride from me again and Evan and I parted ways shortly thereafter. I can't imagine why.

Somewhere along the line, John got my socks and washed them. He actually carried them in his car for a while and continued to promise to get them to me. He never did, but it became a running joke between us. I finally told him not to worry about it and so I would imagine the socks are no more. It was an adventure I'll never forget.

As for the Pikeville Curse, I'll quickly relay two other stories. Regarding the first one, sometime during my two terms my Communications Director, Michael, and I went to Pikeville for me to speak at an event. After stopping at a rest area, and someone commenting on how they liked Michael's car, his car started to have problems. We did get back, but when he took it in to have fixed, it seemed like the cost was several thousand to fix.

The second item was when Agricultural Commissioner Ryan Quarles, Treasurer Allison Ball, and myself flew around the state in a small airplane owned by one of Ryan's friends. This was during our 2019 reelection campaign. One of the stops was in Pikeville. That airport does tend to have difficulties getting into and out of, but as it turned out, everything was fine.

We flew in, did the event in Pikeville, and flew out heading to Butler County, KY. After landing in Butler County, we drove to the event. We all had an opportunity to visit with people there, but I noticed someone came over and whispered into Ryan's ear.

I went over and asked if everything was all right. He indicated some concerns had developed with the plane and we would need to make other arrangements to get back to the airport in Lexington. Thankfully, Ryan was able to coordinate someone to pick us up and get us back to Lexington. During the trip, Ryan was on the phone with his friend who had the plane, and we were relating the Pikeville Curse story. His friend, the pilot, said he was a believer.

As it turned out, they were able to fix the plane, and it actually made it back even before we did in the car. But since we were not sure how long repairs would take, it was important that we hit the road as we had an additional event that night I believe in Mt. Sterling, Kentucky. We were able to make it to all the events, but it was definitely an interesting day.

On the Trail during the 2019 Auditor reelection race
L-R Commisioner Ryan Quarles, Mike (PaPaw), Treasurer Allison Ball

CHAPTER ELEVEN

IT'S NOT EASY BEING OLD

After winning Kentucky Auditor of Public Accounts for the second time in 2019 I found myself in an interesting situation. I became the oldest currently serving Statewide Constitutional Officer in Kentucky at that time by ten years. The closest to my age was our Secretary of State Michael Adams.

So, if anyone knows me, this became a terrific opportunity to find a joke to go along with this condition. My older brother Bobby texted me one shortly after I was sworn in the second time and I was able to adjust to fit the situation perfectly.

The adjusted joke went something like this, "Well, those who know me, know I always like to start with something funny. Today I would like to give you a fact and then give you a funny. Many of you may not know, but I am the oldest currently serving Statewide Constitutional Officer in Kentucky by ten years. Ten years!"

I continued, "The closest one to me is Secretary of State Michael Adams and I'm actually eleven years older than our governor (Andy Beshear.) So, as you can imagine, being the old guy on the block, I might get down from time to time."

Then I would say, "The other day I was looking in the mirror and my lovely bride Lynn, Peaches to our grandchildren since we are Peaches and Papaw, came by and asked me, 'What in the world are you doing?'

Look in that mirror! I look so old, and I look so tired. Can you tell me one good thing about myself, just one to try and pep me or make me feel better? So, she looked and she looked, and she looked, and finally she said, 'well, at least your eyesight is still good.'"

After a moment of pause to allow to sink in with the crowd and a couple of groans as well, I would say, "I'm sorry, I'm sorry! But I guess if you're going to have one good feature as the Auditor, it should be your eyesight."

CHAPTER TWELVE

STAGECOACH JOKE

Over the years I had been known to tell what I called the Stagecoach Joke. It took a couple of different forms over the years, but it generally went something like the following:

"During the time of the old west, there was this fella whose mom needed an operation. So, he looked through the newspaper and tried to find a job. As it turned out there was one for someone to be a shotgun driver on a stagecoach.

He goes and applies, and they asked him, 'Are you sure you want to do this?'

And he responded, 'Yes, my mom needs an operation, so I got to have the money.'

'Ok then,' said the stagecoach driver. 'What you need to do is there is usually a bandit that pops up over the hill while I'm driving. When you see him, let me know how far back he is.'

'Well, I don't know much about distance,' explained the man.

'Ok, then. Just tell me how big he looks,' explained the driver. So, they get to going and the driver says, 'Do you see anything yet?'

'Not yet'
'What about now?'
'I think I see him."
'How big does he look?'
'About this big.' (I would hold my hands about a foot apart.)
'What about now?'
'About this big.' (I would hold my hands about two feet apart.)
'What about now?'
'About this big.' (I would hold my hands about three to four feet apart.)

'What about now?'

'He's right behind us!'

'Well then shoot him!' says the driver.

'I can't shoot him!' says the man.

'You got to shoot him!' says the driver.

'I can't shoot him!' says the man.

'Why can't you shoot him?"

(Placing my hands back to the one-foot apart position.) 'Well, I've known him since he was this big,' says the man."

I would go onto say, "I want to be 100% clear. I am definitely not encouraging anyone to shoot anyone. What I am saying figuratively is that there are multiple programs out there that have seen their time and now need to have the plug pulled on them. Unfortunately, once a government program is created, it is rarely cancelled. The best you can hope for is to cap and contain its growth."

OH! WHAT TO DO! JOKE FOR THE FAITHFUL

I tend to pick up a lot of my jokes from pastors along the way. They are always clean, and they generally create a tie into a message. The next joke I picked up from my very own pastor, Choe Sargent.

There was this pastor of a small rural church who wanted to paint the church since it was in desperate need of a new coat of paint. Unfortunately, the church coffers had been inadequate to hire someone to paint. So, the pastor decided to do it himself. However, he didn't have enough paint to cover the entire church, so he decided to cut the paint with water.

He painted the entire church, and it looked great! He was so proud of himself. But then some clouds started to roll in and it looked like it was going to rain. He knew if it rained before the diluted paint fully dried, it would wash all his work away.
So, he hit his knees and prayed hard. "God what shall I do, what shall I do? The clouds opened up and he heard God respond, "Repaint, Repaint, and thin no more."

CHAPTER THIRTEEN

THEY THOUGHT WHAT ABOUT MY JOKE?

In the course of various jokes and campaign stops, sometimes the jokes I tell may be interpreted by others as having a meaning I did not realize and one I most definitely would not have assigned to it.

One such joke was the flower joke. The way I tell the joke now goes something like this:

"You know Valentines Day is almost here (or just passed) and you might also know that I graduated from EKU with a triple major in Math, Statistics, and Theater. That way I know the math, I know the statistics, and what I don't know I just know act like I know. It works well in politics.

So, I'm really big into statistics and the other day my wife and I were watching a television show and they said that 75% of men don't know their wife's favorite flower and I thought that was ridiculous!

I turn to my wife and say, 'It's all purpose? Right?'"

That's how I tell the joke now. However, for the longest time, I had a different punch line, and it went like this. "So, I turn to my wife and say, It's self-rising? Right?'"

Now you would think it wouldn't matter what baking flour punch line you would use for the joke. But after telling that joke for several months, my friend Congressman Guthrie happened to be in the crowd. He approached me afterwords and said, "That was a funny joke, but I never imagined you of all people would tell something that risqué."

For those who know me, I may have done well in school because of my hard work, and many might consider me above average, but I was far from super smart like some of my friends who made 33 to 35 on their ACT's. However, I have been accused over the years of being a bit naive.

This was one of those situations. After giving some thought to what the Congressman was alluding to without coming right out and saying it, I did switch the punch line. I have had a few tell me since then that although the joke is still funny, it was not as funny as before. However, I did not want anyone to read something into my joke that I did not intend.

Another joke that had a similar concern, but my staff allowed me to tell for a year was the cannibal joke. This was a joke I picked up from another state representative along the way.

When I told it originally, probably for several years before being elected to Auditor and about a year after, it went like this:

"There was this gentleman who traveled the world and one day he happened to wander into a cannibal bar. He thought this is crazy. I've never seen a cannibal bar before.

It looked like a coffee shop with prices written in chalk on a board. $25 for a missionary, $50 for a teacher, $75 for a construction worker, and $150 for a politician.

The gentleman just couldn't resist asking. He waved over the man behind the counter and asked. 'I don't understand. The missionary is $25, but the politician is $150? Why is the politician $150?'

The man behind the counter leans over and says, 'Have you ever tried to clean one of them before?'"

Now I thought that was a funny joke, but I never considered that some individuals might read something else into it until one day at a speaking event, one of my staff leans over to me and says, "The Young Republicans really perked up when you told that joke."

I asked my staffer, "What do you mean?"

"When you got to the part about the missionary, they started smiling and became very focused on where you were going with the joke."

"I don't understand?" I said.

"When you got to the part about the missionary," they repeated.

"Oh, my," I said.

"How long have you known about this response?" I asked.

"For about a year," they responded.

"And you couldn't have let me know before now?"

They smiled and said, "I thought you would figure it out."

After that time when I would tell the joke I would change missionary to minister so as to hopefully minimize the chance of someone reading something into my joke that was not there.

CHAPTER FOURTEEN

IS THERE A REPUBLICAN IN THE HOUSE?

For years I told a joke that unfortunately was based on a true story. As you may recall, the county I live in, Boyle County, was only about 25% registered Republican when I first started campaigning in 1998. In addition, after I won the first time for state representative in 2002 after losing my first two races, I became the first Republican from Boyle County to be elected State Representative in 102 years.

For years I told the same joke about Boyle County. "Boyle County is so bad that the only Republican elected countywide down in a partisan political position is the coroner, and that's only to declare the Republican party dead on arrival in Boyle."

Sad to say I was able to tell that same accurate joke until 2018 when the Republican party finally started to win some partisan races in the county.

Then I had to change to, "Boyle County was so bad that the only Republican elected countywide down in a partisan political position up until 2018 was the coroner, and that was only to declare the Republican party dead on arrival in Boyle."

I told that joke because although Boyle might vote Republican for a federal office or maybe even a State Senator, it rarely voted Republican on the county level and since the 54th House District was only Boyle and Washington Couties (both which only had about a 25% Republican registration) the uphill battle I faced was significant. But my hard headedness and determination thankfully was significant as well and I am thankful God eventually blessed me with a victory.

ARE THERE ANY MORE REPUBLICANS OUT THERE?

When I first arrived in Frankfort in 2003 after winning in the 2002 race, I believe the Republicans only had thirty-six members out of one hundred in the House. Because of this fact and because the Democrat party did not want me to have anything to campaign on, the only bill I was able to pass that I was the primary sponsor on was a House Joint Resolution to codify a county line between Boyle and Lincoln that had been agreed to and was wanted by our Democrat Judge Executive. And my friend, former colleague, and chief of staff as Auditor teased me that it didn't count as a bill since it was a resolution.

Now don't misunderstand. There were many bills that had the DNA of what I wanted in a bill to pass, but I had to work with a state senator in the Republican controlled State Senate and a Democrat State Representative in the House. I was not the first to say it, but I always said if you don't worry about who gets credit, then you can get a lot accomplished.

This philosophy was helpful when we passed the Christine Talley Act. While in the House, a friend of mine called me about his mother. She had one of the personal monitors (help I've fallen, and I can't get up) that unfortunately when she pushed the button, and they couldn't get a response from Mrs. Talley they went through a list of numbers trying to get ahold of people on her contact list. By the time they had called that list and then eventually got to 911, it was too late.

Jim had arrived at his mother's house sometime during that time, but unfortunately it was too late. He genuinely believed that if they had called 911 first when they couldn't get a response from Mrs. Talley that his mother would have still been alive.

Because of his passion on this issue, he reached out to me and asked if I would pass a bill to require these types of companies to call 911 first if the request button is pushed but there is no response from the customer when they communicate back.

I agreed to have a bill drafted and invited him to visit with me and a bill drafter. He went much further than that. He pulled together multiple stake holders including EMS. I worked with some of the legislative agents who had concerns and together we drafted a bill that we all thought would have a positive impact in preventing or minimizing something like this from happening again.

My counterpart in the Senate, Senator Tom Buford also drafted a bill but the DNA of his bill was different from mine and Jim was more interested in the bill we had worked on together.

Tom was able to get his bill passed out of the Senate and it came over to the House. I reached out to Tom and asked if we could amend his bill to mirror the bill Jim and I had worked on together. He was very agreeable, but we still had one more hurdle.

Because I was a Republican in the minority and one that was always at risk of being beaten in the next cycle, Democrats would not let me have this win in my name. Instead, I worked with a reasonably conservative Democrat, Representative Bob Dameron, and after a few tweaks to our version, he agreed to carry the amendment to Tom's bill on the floor of the House.

We were getting close to the session being concluded so I went with Jim over to the Senate to try and get the Senate to concur with our amendment. The Senate Majority Floor Leader, Dan Kelly, waved me over and asked what our amendment did and asked if Tom was ok with it. I explained it and said Tom was ok. Dan then called it up, the amendment was adopted, and the bill became law.

Jim was ecstatic and thanked me for making sure it made it through the process. I'd like to take credit, and I did help, but it was Jim's determination and desire that got this bill written and passed in one session. I had never seen a bill go from concept to completion in such a rapid manner.

Jim even went as far as to get me an award from AARP for the legislation which I thought was funny since I was not the primary sponsor, nor did I officially carry the amendment that contained the DNA we wanted for the bill. It only goes to show as I said that if you don't worry about who gets credit, you can get a lot done.

During my entire time in the House, I was always, always in the minority. The funny thing was after I won Auditor in 2015, the next full election cycle the Republicans took control of the House not only with a Majority, but with a super Majority.

I always said if I knew I was the one holding them back, I would have left years ago.

CHAPTER FIFTEEN

STRING MUSIC

One joke that I used on the trail I have to give credit to my Mother-in-Law. I heard her tell this joke one time and I have dubbed it the string joke and it goes like this:

"There were these three strings, a big string, a middle string, and a little string. And these three strings decided they wanted to go get a beer. (Root beer if speaking with minors.)

So, the big string goes into the bar and pounds on the counter, and says, 'Bartender, give me a beer.'

The bartender leans over and says, 'Err you be a string?'

The big string says, 'Why yes I am.'

The bartender says, 'Get out of here! We don't serve any strings!'

The big string heads out with his head held low and goes out to tell the others what happened.

The middle string says, 'That's not right! I'm going in there and get a beer.'

So, the middle string storms in and pounds his fist on the counter and says, 'Bartender, give me a beer!'

The bartender leans over and says, 'Err you be a string?'

The middle string responds, 'Why yes I am.'

The bartender says, 'Get out of here! We don't serve any strings!'

So, the Middle String heads out and with his head hanging down and goes tells the other strings.

Now the Small String is somewhat humble, but he says, 'I'll go try.' The Small String combs his hair down and ties himself into a bow. Then he goes into the bar, walks up to the counter and says, 'B. . . B... Bartender, c. . . can I have a beer, please?'

The bartender leans over and asks, 'Err you be a string?'

The Little String responds, 'No sir, I'm a frayed knot.'"

Now once again after saying, "I'm sorry. I'm sorry." I usually go on to tie it unto something like, "When the Democrats want to take more of your money by raising your taxes, what are we going to tell them? I'm a frayed knot.

When someone says an unborn child has no value and is not a life, what are we going to tell them? I'm a frayed knot."

These types of comparisons would go on for 3 or 4 stanzas before I would head onto the main body of the story that I would continue to tie to this analogy.

THE PROMISES WE MAKE

After getting elected to State Representative for the first time in 2002, my wife and I decided to take a Dave Ramsey course at our church. I became so motivated to get out of debt that before the 13-week class was even over, I took an extra job delivering pizza.

Unfortunately, this left my wife alone in most of the remaining classes each week as I delivered pizza, but I would listen to the tapes as I drove around. I was so excited to follow the program.

As I delivered a pizza to one house, someone looked at me and paused. Then they said, "Hey aren't you our new State Representative?"

I quickly replied back, "Yes, and during my campaign, I promised to deliver. So here I am."

He smiled and headed back in.

THE AUDITOR'S DOG

During my time as Auditor, I spoke to many different groups and as always, I usually would start with something funny. However, whenever I spoke with the Internal Auditors group, my jokes never seemed to land. They were in fact a very tough crowd.

Though I usually have borrowed (or appropriated) most of my jokes, I decided to write a joke that would be more of an inside joke that would generally be better understood by auditors, accountants and anyone who had been audited. I did just that and so when I went back to speak to the Internal Auditors, this is the joke I told:

"Did you hear about the auditor that was very concerned about his pet dog?"

"His dog would use the bathroom at the exact same location every single time."

"So, the auditor was very concerned about a lack of segregation of duties."

Now to the average individual, that joke might not seem funny, but auditors loved that joke as it took a finding that is quite common in audits, "Lack of Segregation of Duties," and did a play on words of the dog pooping in the exact same spot. And yes, the Internal Auditors did chuckle which did my heart good.

WE'RE GOING TO HELP YOU OUT

Now after getting elected for the first time a PAC (Political Action Committee) representing the beer wholesalers wanted to meet with me at McDonald's in Danville to give me a PAC check for my next campaign. As was my usual policy, I would meet with anyone regardless of whether they supported me or not.

I can't remember if I ate anything that day, but it was always my policy when meeting with just about everyone but definitely anyone that might be trying to influence me that I would buy my own meal or even a drink to avoid a conflict. The General Assembly did have some exceptions regarding receptions that all legislators were invited to, but it was a safe bet for one on one's to buy your own meals.

During that meeting, the gentleman slid over an envelope that he said had a PAC check in it (which is perfectly legal) but I slid it back over to him.

I explained that I was very appreciative, but our county had just gone through a series of votes to make parts of the county moist (a term used to allow the limited sale of adult beverages in some restaurants), and I had taken the remain dry side of the argument in the community.

Now I don't mind if someone has a drink if they are responsible, but I and others in the county had multiple concerns about the expansion of alcohol into the area. The dry side was only partially successful as the vote in Junction City had failed at that time, but Danville was able to pass the vote on moist.

As a side note, the funny thing about the first time I was elected was when many of these votes were taking place and had even been an issue at some of my debates and door to door. I told my wife the night of the election that even though I would be the first Republican to be elected to this position from Boyle County in 102 years, my guess was that either it would not be on the front page or if my victory was it would be a very small portion of it.

Needless to say, I was correct. My victory was on the front page, but it only took up maybe five to ten percent of the page. The majority of front page covered "Danville Goes Wet (or Moist)"

But to get back to the topic of my meeting, after I slid the check back, the gentleman from the Beer Wholesaler PAC told me that he understood and that they truly appreciated my position on the bottle bill.

The bottle bill was a bill that House Majority Floor Leader Greg Stumbo had been trying to pass for years. Basically, it assessed deposits on bottles and cans as well as a ½ cent tax on every disposable cup used in fast food restaurants. It was sold under the idea that monies collected could be used to help clean up trash and illegal dumps.

Oddly enough, in a previous debate with Bill Erwin, one of my supporters brought up the question as to whether I supported the bill because she thought it was a good idea. I had to explain that though I appreciated her position, I could not support it because it was an additional tax, and we did not need to tax citizens any more than currently.

When the question was proposed to my opponent for that race, Bill Erwin, he indicated that he supported and hoped it could pass. Now when Bill said he supported it, my former opponent who had beaten me twice (and my only Democrat opponent I never beat,) John Bowling's eyes got wide as plates.

You see, John owned several fast-food restaurants that he had built up over the years (as he had started from humble beginnings) and had always fought with Greg Stumbo over the years. After that, I always felt like I had John's support, at least behind the scenes and years later he confirmed that suspicion.

But once again back to the gentleman from the PAC. As I said, he said they appreciated my position on the bottle bill and would "Help Me Out" in other ways. Well, as it turned out, they ended up donating $1,000 (the max at that time) to my opponent.

At the time it happened, I told this story to my good friend and fellow Freshman Legislator Jimmy Higdon. He just laughed and said, "Son, you weren't listening to them. They said they were going to 'help you out.'" He did the motion of someone pushing a person out the door.

It turned out that it didn't matter anyway as God continued to bless me with victories. I imagine there may have been individuals who saw that donation on my opponent's report and decided to go with me.

However, it did give me a great joke and story to tell over the years much to the chagrin of the PAC which it referenced. Interestingly, I told that story to the chair of the Banking and Insurance Committee, Jim Bruce, who had been around for decades. He told me to listen closely. To paraphrase, he said what you need to do is just wait. And then sometime when they really needed something to gig them. Well, as you imagine, that really wasn't my style, but I did think it was interesting coming from a high-level, old-school Democrat. I may not have agreed with him on everything, but I appreciated the time he took to mentor those he liked regardless of their party.

YOUR WIFE COMES FROM A GOOD FAMILY.

During my second race for State Representative a few people in the local Republican Party talked my wife into running for city council in Junction City, Kentucky. This created a couple of interesting events.

First, my wife was not much on campaigning, but she did walk a street or two. I'm not really sure she wanted to run but she was willing to take one for the team (The Team being our local Republican Party) even if it was a non-partisan race.

During that time, I was also aggressively campaigning for State Representative (for the second time.) As I was walking the streets of Junction City, I ran into one gentleman who we had a good conservation.

At the end of our visiting, he said, "I'm sorry but I can't vote for you." Certainly, I understood as Boyle was close to 75% registered Democrat. But then he followed with, "But I'll vote for your wife. She comes from a good family." Now I wasn't sure if I or maybe my Mom was supposed to be mad, but I accepted the vote on behalf of my wife and went on my way.

As it turned out on election night, though my wife had barely campaigned she came in second of all those running for city council and that was sufficient for her to have a victory. I unfortunately lost my second race for State Representative.

My wife Lynn could tell that I was a bit despondent, and she came over to try and comfort me. She said, "Hey, it's ok, Honey. I only came in second too." Of course, I responded back, "Yeah, but yours counted."

That was a tough race. It was the second time I had run and the 2nd I had run against John Bowling. When I lost, I lost by less than 200 votes so it may have hurt even more than my first race. But God still had something he wanted me to do.

OH, WHAT BIG EYES YOU HAVE!

I remember when our youngest, Lizzie, was around three, my wife stayed home with her while I was at work. One day for some reason Lynn was talking about the assorted colors of our families' eyes.

She said, " . . . Now you have brown eyes and Daddy has hazel brown eyes."

A little while later, Lizzie got on the phone with my Mom and she was recounting what she had learned, ". . . Mommy has brown eyes, and I have brown eyes, and Daddy has weasel brown eyes."

I'm not certain, but maybe that was a prediction that I would become a politician, LOL.

CHAPTER SIXTEEN

PROTESTORS YOU SAY?

Over the years I have seen a lot of protests. Perhaps the one I remember the most occurred during the year and a half that I was in San Diego, California, between 1995 and 1996. I had noticed that Newt Gingrich was going to be in town for a book signing and I decided I would go, buy his book, and have him autograph it.

When I arrived, there was a small group of protestors sitting out front. They had signs but most were pretty tame, and several of them were just sitting down. Before I headed into the signing, a reporter pulled up and went over to address the group.

"Let's gin this thing up," I heard the reporter say. Next, they all stood up and started waving their signs while hollering at people. I knew it was ok to protest, but at that time I didn't think about the press coordinating the intensity.

I went on in, stood in line, and eventually got my book signed and had a brief conversation with The Speaker. I can't really remember what he said now, but he seemed nice enough.

As I went outside to head back to my car, someone shoved a sign in my face that said, "Newt Gingrich, DEADBEAT DAD!" Now, I really wasn't sure what they were talking about, but for some reason I quipped back with a smile, "Well, at least he allowed his child to be born."

The crowd was not pleased as you can imagine, so I headed on as quickly as I could with the satisfaction that I had held my own, and maybe (but probably not) had caused some in the crowd to reconsider their positions.

That event taught me the important lesson that often things are staged more for the press than necessarily for the effectiveness of that day. It was kind of a sad lesson that over the years I have seen grow only worse as people not only protest, but also turn to violence. Though the press rarely admits to it, those type of events are much more likely on the Liberal/Progressive side than the Conservative side.

Hopefully, that will change one day, and we can have honest conversation and debate without demonizing and relying on violence. But I feel it may take another sad and catastrophic event to force us to come together. I just pray I am wrong on this issue.

CHAPTER SEVENTEEN

YOU GOT TO HAVE A LITTLE RED TRUCK TO BE STATE REPRESENTATIVE!

It was interesting that I believe the two state representatives that preceded me from Boyle County including John Bowling and Joe Clarke both had little red trucks. As it turned out, when my Dad passed, he had just bought in the last 6 months prior to his passing a little red truck.

The truck was a stick shift so Mom could not drive it. Since we could use an additional vehicle, I offered to buy it from my Mom and set up a financing plan with her that included me paying interest.

When I bought it, I checked under the seat and my Dad had three cartons of cigarettes, Marlboro, that had sat under his seat for at least 6 months. Dad had tried to quit smoking before he died and did quit smoking in the house and around Mom but apparently, he had not quit completely.

I ended up giving the cartons to one of our assistant managers at Trim Masters who worked on the night shift who smoked them when he ran out of his others. He said Marlboro is strong anyway, but when they set in the truck for six months, they are very strong. I asked him why he didn't throw them away, but he was like, "Are you kidding, those things are expensive."

The little red truck served me well. It saw many a parade. It also almost had or witnessed some casualties. Well, kind of anyway.

I remember one time, State Senator, Dan Kelly, was riding in the back with me as my wonderful wife, Lynn, was driving the truck. Unfortunately, she popped the clutch too quickly and almost threw the good senator out of the truck. Thankfully, he did not fall, and he did not get injured. I don't recall him riding with us again after that, but he may have. At least we had a good story, and no one got hurt.

MY LITTLE RED TRUCK
LOVED A PARADE.

"He's got Pez!" Junction City Parade
Truck Bed: L-R Mike, Ben McClain. Cab: Lynn

On another occasion, while my wife drove and my Mom rode in the cab and I was in the back waving to the crowd and throwing candy, there was an Elvis impersonator in front of us. He was doing all sorts of dancing and Lynn and Mom got tickled and almost lost control of the truck. Thankfully, they did not hit the impersonator, but it was a close call.

Finally, my opponent, John Bowling, hopped onto a tractor in front of us during another parade. Instead of having someone drive, he decided he wanted to drive himself and wanted to carry a flag at the same time. When he started, he lost control for a moment and almost ran off the road. Thankfully neither he nor anyone in the crowd was hurt.

Also, word of advice, if you are posting about your "little red truck" make sure it doesn't say "little read truck." I did that once and thankfully it did not stay posted too long before I caught and switched out. I suppose if my truck could read it might be accurate, but I never took the time to teach it.

One time I spoke to Mom's kindergarten class and a student asked me if I had ever been in a parade. I responded yes and that by that time I had probably been in a 150 or more. His eyes got so wide, and he smiled. I assume that was impressive for him.

As I said, that was a good little truck. I still have it, but it has long since been retired from parades. It's a bit beat up and has a different engine from the original, but I have a hard time parting with it. I still use it if we need to move something close by or haul something to the dump.

Mom always says she's glad she let my Dad buy the truck. He was so proud of it even if he only had it for a few months before he died. I think every man needs a pickup truck and I'm glad I was able to buy Dad's after he passed.

"HE'S GOT PEZS"

As was mentioned in the discussion about my "Little Red Truck," we participated in a lot of community parades. We would, as was customary, toss out candy to the crowd. We did this for years until one community decided not to allow it for fear a child would run in front of a vehicle (which did happen in one of their parades but thankfully the child was not hurt).

However, for years, I did toss out candy and there are many stories related to that process, but I will focus on two of the more memorable ones. During one occasion, I was tossing out candy at a parade in Springfield, Kentucky when I realized I was going to and did run out of candy. I looked around in the back of the truck and noticed my briefcase.

Why it was there, I don't recall; however, when I opened it up, I noticed a stack of refrigerator magnets with my information on them. I decided to start tossing them out. The kids seemed to love the magnets. But then the wind caught one of them and hit a women smack dab in the middle of her forehead.

I'm thinking I did not get that vote. But thankfully I was not sued or anything worse happened.

During one parade, I obtained candy from a friend who was a candy broker and who had some of the best candy out there. Luckily, he had lots of left-over samples. One of the things I got from him was Pez candy and dispensers.

My opponent who was also in the parade was tossing out the small individual peppermint candies. All of sudden I heard a kid yell, "He's got Pez's!" Needless to say, a large crowd of kids started heading my way and I was the hit of that parade at least with the kids.

Parades were fun and I will always have fond memories of those events.

CHAPTER EIGHTEEN

SPEAKING WITH FOURTH GRADERS IS TRICKY

During my time in the KY General Assembly, I would enjoy going into classes and speaking with students of all ages. Sometimes I would bring a video and curriculum prepared by NCSL (National Conference of State Legislators), but I always tried to give them a feel of what it was like to be a Legislator.

What I would usually do is to say to the class, "Ok, today you all are all House Members." Then I would select a smaller group and say, "This group will be the Favorites Committee."

Now we didn't have a Favorites Committee in Frankfort, but I thought it might be an effective way to help them understand. Then I would pick someone from the committee, usually one of the shyer people, and make them the Chair of the Favorites Committee.

I would then say to the class, "Ok, what's a category we want to do favorites?" Favorite sports teams? Favorite Food?"

After we had a category, I would encourage the class to nominate their favorite in that category. For sports, you almost always had UK or sometimes UK and Louisville. Sometimes we did favorite food which generally had pizza, chicken, etc.

Then I would turn to the chairman or madame chairman and ask, "You have the power. The committee can vote on all these bills, some of these bills, or none of these bills."

Amazingly, the chairman would act much like we experienced in Frankfort. Some would allow all favorite nomination bills to be voted on. Some would allow only the ones they wanted, and some would allow only their nomination. I did have to remind them if a bill made it out of committee and then was voted on favorably by the full House (class), we would stop the process (because really you can only have one favorite in a category.)

If a bill was found favorable by the committee, then it would go to the full House for a vote and if it received a majority vote, it would move on through the process. Although I explained it would normally have to go through the Senate process as well, signed, allowed to become law without his/her signature or vetoed by the governor, and then the possibility of a veto override, for our purposes once it passed the House, it would be considered law (in the class anyway.)

Classes loved this, but I learned you have to be careful with younger kids, especially fourth graders. In one such class they decided to nominate their favorite toys.

The nominations came in and I wrote them on the board. Once bill filings were complete, I turned to the Chair and asked her which bills she would consider? She was methodical so first she decided to eliminate the toys she would not even consider.

As each toy was denied the opportunity for a vote, I would erase them from the board. As I erased one particular toy, the fourth grader who had nominated that toy broke down in tears. We paused to comfort him, but then had to proceed with the process.

When I retell this story to other classes, I have to relate that being in the minority all my years in the House, I can certainly understand how the young man felt. It is a good lesson for life that you can't always get what you want at the time, but you also can't let that get you down. If the issue is profoundly important, then you must seek other avenues to accomplish your goal in that area.

CHAPTER NINETEEN

HOW EMBARRASSING!

After winning in 2002, I had the honor of being sworn in on the first day of the 2003 Session in January. Since this would be my first swearing in, I had multiple family members who had played a role in my election, especially several of my great aunts and uncles and cousins from Washington County who wanted to be present on that day.

I believe I had around twenty people there including my Mother. Typically, you would only be afforded two tickets for guests in the Gallery, but for several members this was not their first swearing in, so I was given enough tickets for all my family.

The day was extremely exciting, and Legislators were all sworn in together. Then Legislators were given the opportunity to introduce their guests. I wasn't really sure what was going on, but Representative (now State Senator) Brandon Smith leaned over and pushed my RTS (request to speak) button and said when they call on you introduce your guest.

Needless to say, I was nervous and never considered I might be introducing guests. Then I heard the Speaker say something to the effect of, "For what does the Gentleman from Boyle 54 seek recognition?"

I spoke into the microphone, and carefully introduced each of my guests, asked for them to be welcomed and everyone applauded. Feeling good about my first major speaking test, I sat down and then after the Speaker had gone onto the next Legislator, a horrible feeling began to come over me. I realized that yes, I had successfully introduced all of my guests, all that is but one.

I had forgotten to introduce the one woman that brought me into this world. I had forgotten to introduce my Mom. If I had been thinking, I could have pushed my RTS button again and corrected my oversight, but I was so green and originally had not even given consideration to introducing anyone. I failed to complete the mission and had to live with the consequences at lunch and for years to come.

Now my Mom is not one to make a big deal about such an incident, but I could tell she was noticeably hurt, and I was sad I had failed to recognize her. Over the next several years, she would tease me about it and although it was a teasing there seemed to be at least under the surface) a small bit of sadness in the teasing. For that mistake I will forever be sorry because I love Mom very much and would never want to hurt her.

In the process of writing this book I was reviewing election night videos including my 2015 and 2019 Auditor victories. In 2015, the video was clear that I had recognized in addition to my wife, Lynn, my girls, my son-in-law, and others, I did also recognize my Mom.

However, in reviewing the 2019 election night coverage, videos I found initially were already in progress and so it appeared I had failed to introduce my Mom once again. I began to think did I forget her again and suppress that all these years. Thankfully, I did eventually find a video that included all or at least most of my speech and it did include at the beginning a thank you to my Mom, my Lord and Savior, Jesus Christ, and my earthly Father who had passed on years earlier in addition to my normal recognitions.

I am so thankful for my Mom and hope that she is with us for many more years, and I hope to never forget her again.

CHAPTER TWENTY

THAT TIME GOD CRUSHED AND HUMBLED ME TO PREPARE ME

Years ago, after college, I worked at a couple of finance companies and a buy here pay here. At these types of companies, you saw the entire financial and personal spectrum when it came to people. You met some of the best and some of the worst people. You visited people who you wondered why they were here when it was obvious they could obtain financing at a bank. And you met people who you definitely knew why they were there.

Now one particular time I was visiting with a couple at a finance company looking to obtain a loan. He was a pastor and he and his wife seemed like wonderful people. I took the application and pulled the necessary reports and then I noticed it.

This couple had filed for bankruptcy. I thought to myself and then asked God, why in the world would a professing Christian and a pastor especially ever file for bankruptcy.

Now I didn't know it at the time, but God had listened to my question but had chosen to wait to answer it. A few years later, I left a job at a bank, and I moved my family to California.

I was going to work for my brother-in-law who was married to my wife's sister. He was going to train me on how to do lettering on comic books as well as other items working with comic books and trading cards. I was going to do this and also try my hand at breaking into acting.

In addition to lettering credit in several comic books, I also got a couple of acting jobs. Almost all were extra jobs including an episode of a USA Network detective show, "Silk Stalkings Partners Part II." I was in fifteen to twenty scenes, but it was more like, "Where's Mike"

However, through a series of financial mistakes, I had placed my family in a financial bind. We went to seek credit counseling and though I had hoped they would help us navigate the choppy waters their advice was to file for bankruptcy.

And then the question I had asked years earlier was answered by God. "How can someone who claims to be a Christian file for bankruptcy?" We did go through the process, and it was humbling to say the least.

God had used my arrogance to crush me and humble me. I didn't realize then how he was preparing me. That humbling prepared me to care more about people. The crushing helped me to understand, but by the Grace of God, anyone can be in a similar situation.

We were only in California for about a year and a half and when we returned, we did so with very little money and hat in hand going back to Junction City to live with my Mom and Dad for a month to six weeks before we could find a rundown house to rent and a job to go to.

Oddly enough, it was later that year when I went to vote and realized only one person on the ballot for state representative in 1996 that I began my praying and my pursuit. For some reason in 25 years of running and 21 years of serving, no one ever publicly brought up the bankruptcy. Perhaps God blinded their eyes as not to see that flaw.

I can't say I'm glad I went through it, but I can say I'm glad God used it to mold me and help me to appreciate what others go through in their life. I no longer ask God why a Christian does something. I ask God to help me love the people even if I at times don't feel like it. For that I am grateful.

CHAPTER TWENTY ONE

STATE REPRESENTATIVE WAS NOT YOUR FIRST RACE?

During my time on the trail, I usually talked about how I lost my first two races for State Representative but only rarely talked about my first actual political race that I remember.

One of my teachers in high school, Mr. Best, recommended me to go to Boys State at Eastern Kentucky University in Richmond, Kentucky that year. Boys State simulated state government including electing officials and making mock laws.

As it turned out, there was a young man who talked me into running for governor and apparently, he was very convincing because I did. Once the process for that part was over and the vote was cast, I received two total votes. Mine and what I can only assume was the young man who nominated me.

They ended up making me a state representative so I could still participate in the process, and it was interesting to say the least. However, though I would experience more defeats over the years, apparently that first defeat (as well as the others) did not dissuade me from pursuing what I felt that God was leading me to do in the years to come.

I was thankful for the opportunity Mr. Best provided and was thankful for the experience.

Photo taken after a 2015 KRS Boyle County Remote Broadcast
L-R Matt Jones, Mike (PaPaw)

CHAPTER TWENTY TWO

KSR AND RYAN LEMOND

Over the years, I have enjoyed listening to KSR from time to time. Their primary focus has always been Kentucky sports, but they do at times veer into politics. I don't generally agree with their positions on politics, but I do find them interesting.

During my 2015 race for Auditor, KSR hosted a governor's debate during the primary that I believe was a turning point for Matt Bevin who eventually became the nominee and then won in the fall. Matt Jones of KSR was a good friend of my opponent and incumbent Auditor, Adam Edelen, and Adam had multiple commercials on KSR and Matt commented on them during the show.

I very much wanted to try and have a General Election Debate (neither Adam nor myself had a Primary) on KSR like the governor debate. So, when KSR did an onsite show in Danville, I went to the show, and even tweeted at the show. Matt acknowledged that I was there. After the show I approached Matt and asked if he would be willing to do an Auditor debate.

Matt thanked me for being at the show (and now I'm paraphrasing but basically, he said, "An Auditor debate would be too boring, and we would lose the audience quickly. It would not make for good on-air programming."

So, there was not an auditor debate at KSR. Adam and I had several events together including the one with KET. But not one at KSR. As it turned out, it didn't matter since I still was able to win despite the odds.

The night I won Auditor in 2015, my eldest daughter, Tori, was on stage with Peaches (my wife Lynn) and my first grandson. He was about four and a half months old, and Tori had placed him in a swaddling wrap that she carried in front of her.

Matt Jones and some at KSR were probably still a little sad/mad that their guy Adam had lost, and started making fun of how Tori was carrying our grandchild. To paraphrase, "Does she have a child under her shirt?" They were very fixated on the issue. I wasn't really happy with what they were saying, but I had the victory, and they just needed to grow up.

After I became Auditor, Matt Jones got a local tv show in addition to his radio show. It was called, "Hey Kentucky!"   There were at least two times that one of our audits was mentioned on the show in a positive light.

On one particular audit dealing with Kentucky's Retirement System, Ryan Lemond was extremely excited about the audit my office did and had several great lines like, "Hey, Mike Harmon is dead on! I tell you what, that's my money!" and "Go for it, Mike Harmon! You do you, buddy." "Go for it, Big Fellow." "You do you, Buddy!"

So, I, and my ad team for my reelection thought those lines would work well in a radio ad especially if we ran on KSR since Ryan was a particularly important part of that show and loved by the audience. After a brief discussion, we decided before we used the quotes from the tv program that it would be best if I asked permission from Ryan first.

As it turned out, finding Ryan's number was not a problem since he was also a realtor. I googled his number and gave him a call. I'll be paraphrasing a little, but the call went something like this:

Ryan: "Hello."

Me: "Hi, this is Mike Harmon, how are you doing, Ryan."

Ryan: "Uh. . . fine. You doing ok?"

Me: "Yeah. . . hey I saw where you complimented one of my audits on 'Hey Kentucky' and I was wondering if I could use some quotes from it for my reelection campaign if we ran it on KSR?"
Ryan: "Uh. . . I'm sorry who did you say you were again?"

Me: "I'm Auditor Mike Harmon. Kentucky's Auditor of Public Accounts."

Ryan: "Oh, thank goodness. Yes, that would be fine."

Ryan went on to explain that when he first picked up, he thought I was the principal of his son's school who just happened to also be named Mike Harmon. He indicated he was so relieved that I was the Auditor. It might have been the first time I got that response.

We did use his quotes for a 60-second radio ad that we played on KSR and other radio stations. It first aired on October 23, 2019 while I was headed to Pikeville for an event and making a few stops on the way.

As it turned out, during the show, Matt stopped and was like, "The world has officially gone insane." Then they took the time to play the beginning of it several times on the show and teased Ryan. Matt said, "It sounds like you're calling Mike Harmon, 'Your Money.'

This went on and off for (really) the rest of the entire show. Somewhere during the show, they also talked about my opponent, Sheri Donahue, and asked Ryan if he would also do an ad for her. He said sure.

I called into the show and was joking about what did I do to lose Ryan's support. I promised I could do better. Then Sheri called in and they joked with her also. It was a great and fun day, and I believe the ad definitely helped with my reelection.

Several years later, when I was running for governor, I got invited to the KSR governors' debate. It was great fun but what I enjoyed the most was the opportunity to tell a joke and so I told the Clarence joke.

I received a standing ovation from Drew Franklin and Shannon the Dude. Matt was just like, "That's terrible." It was a great event, and they had promoted me leading up to the debate on one day using the "Follow the Data" line including asking callers to work the line into their questions.

I know we probably don't agree on politics, but I am thankful and appreciative of the friendship with those at KSR and especially Ryan Lemmond. It was really fun getting to know them.

During the 2019 Auditor reelection race. L-R President Trump, Mike (PaPaw)

CHAPTER TWENTY THREE

GOVERNOR'S RACE, MARK/MIKE, AND TRUMP IN MY COMMERCIAL

After being reelected to Auditor, I began to pray about a run for governor. I was trying to figure out whether I was going to run for treasurer or governor or not at all.

In Kentucky, you can only be elected to two consecutive terms as any of the Statewide Constitutional Officers, and so I would have to figure out after the next few years what direction God would have me go. The easiest path would have been to have run for Treasurer and though not a guarantee, I would have been the favorite and possibly could have cleared the field had I announced earlier.

My wife says if there is a hard path to take, I can usually find it and unfortunately, she is correct. However, I did want to pray about and follow the direction I felt God was leading me.

After prayerful consideration, I did decide to run for governor despite my concerns with past fundraising and the fact that I had never won a primary. Up until the race for governor I had only had one Primary in all my years of running.

I joke now that after I termed out as Auditor, I had run 25 years, served twenty-one years straight, and yet had never won a primary. Technically I only had two primaries but if you include someone talking me into running for party chair at the last minute and losing that, you could say three.

For the most part, over the years, I was more of a Don Quixote candidate. I would usually run in races that no other Republican thought could be won. I jokingly say the conversation goes something like this:

Person 1 to Person 2: "You want to run for. . . "

Person 2 to Person 1: "I don't want to run."

Person 2 to Person 1: "Do you want to run?"

Person 1 to Person 2: "I don't want to run. Hey let's get Mikey. He'll run for anything."

Well, it really wasn't that bad and usually what happened was I'd see a situation where there was a void, I'd pray about it and then I would run. After losing to John Bowling those first two times, I've never lost to a Democrat since 2000.

But, in the case of the 2023 Republican Primary for Governor, there was a total of twelve candidates in the race and at least 4 or 5 were either well off or at least were connected enough to raise the needed funds to run. I, unfortunately, was neither.

Before all of the twelve got in, I was speaking with a friend in Western Kentucky and I told him of everyone in the race (at that time) I was the oldest, the most experienced, and the funniest. He looked right back and me and quipped, "two out of three ain't bad."

I'll cut to the end so I can go back to the middle. After over two years of running for governor (yes, I started very early) and only raising about $85,000, I came in fifth out of those twelve with three percent (you have to round up to get to three percent.)

As you can imagine, that was pretty crushing. But I still felt as if running for governor was the direction God wanted me to go. I don't know why but His Will be done, and I pray that was in fact His Will.

Getting back to the middle, I had a fantastic opportunity to meet some more wonderful people and build additional friendships. One such friendship was a young couple who wanted to help me put together some campaign videos.

Since she was just starting her new business, we sat down and negotiated a price that was acceptable with my limited budget and the fact she was wanting to work on her video skills. Her husband helped her, when possible, but he also had another job elsewhere and this was her business. They were and are an extremely sweet couple and it was an honor to get to know them both on the trail.

She did several videos that we used on Facebook, and they were all great, but my favorite was the last one she did that we released about a week before the election. This video had a sweet older lady from my church who I had known for years and was friends with her children.

The video played on something I have faced my entire life even before politics where instead of calling me Mike Harmon, they call me Mark Harmon. I think it's because the names are similar, and Mark Harmon is a famous actor. He's better looking and makes more money than me so I'm not sure why people get us confused.

This sweet lady and I were sitting on a bench, and she would say something close to "I'm here with Mark Harmon and he's running for governor." Then I would say, "Yes ma'am. But it's Mike Harmon."

Then she would start another line, "Marty Harmon is endorsed by. . .," followed with me going, "Yes ma'am. But it's Mike Harmon."
Finally at the end she says, "And even Trump knows his name." Then I just shrugged "Hmm?" After, we show a video of President Trump at a 2019 Rally in Kentucky introducing me as "Auditor Mark Harmon. (Clapping) Thank you, Mark."

The camera cuts back to me and I whisper, "But it's Mike Harmon." And the sweet lady pats my leg and says, "Yes, Dear." It was a great commercial and I only wished I had had more money to run it even more. I've included the link.

Mark/Mike Commercial: Mike Harmon for Governor
https://www.youtube.com/watch?v=x7kv0NyFeQE

During the 2019 Auditor Race President Trump signs a "Keep Auditing Great" hat for me.
Top L-R President Trump, Mike (PaPaw) Bottom L-R Michael Adams, Mike (PaPaw),
Congressman Guthrie, Treasurer Ball, Commissioner Quarles,
Leader McConnell, State Senator Alvarado, Daniel Cameron.

Screen grab of the funniest commercial ever during my race for Governor.
L-R Mike (PaPaw), Ramona Kendrick

Running for governor was, as I said, a wonderful experience. I wish I had gotten better at raising funds and had won, but I know God had a reason for me going through this fire and hopefully someday I will understand.

THAT TIME WE ERASED MY YOUNGER BROTHER.

As was mentioned, during my race for governor, there was someone who was trying to improve their video making skills and so we struck a deal on costing and proceeded to record a few videos. All were good, but the first was a reflection through my Mom's house including some old photos.

One of those photos was of my Mom, my Dad, my older brother and myself. My younger brother, Tony, had not been born at the time of the photo and the video did not include one of him in it.

When the video came out, it had some great reviews, but my younger brother texted me and my older brother. Unlike when I forgot to introduce my Mom, we found this a bit humorous.

There was a great deal of teasing back and forth and others who noted they were missing also, but everyone was in fact ok.

L-R Sister-in-Laws Missy & Deidra, Niece Matrie, Lynn, Lizzie, Mom (MaMaw Janet)

Top L-R Janet (Mike's Mom/ MaMaw Janet), Darrell (Mike's Dad), Bottom L-R Mike, Brother Bobby

Bottom Photo:
Mike & his brothers
L-R Bobby, Mike (PaPaw), and Tony

CHAPTER TWENTY FOUR

SORRY. . . NOTHING TO SEE HERE

When you are a sitting Constitution Officer, there are tremendous opportunities for growth. One of those was going to our party's national convention. In 2016, I went to the Republican National Convention in Cleveland, Ohio.

There were wonderful events that attendees had an opportunity to visit. On one particular day, I had decided to stay back at the hotel so I could catch up on some work and I ended up running into a newly found friend from Kentucky and he indicated he and his family were heading over to The Rock & Roll Hall of Fame and asked if I would like to join them.

I had finished my work and accepted his offer, and we headed that way. We did get a chance to visit the Hall of Fame, but while inside, we found out that Trump was flying in and was going to address those who were there outside.

We headed outside and noticed that there was, as expected, a screening process to go through before we could go in. If I remember correctly, my friend had press credentials, so he was able to take a different path into the event.

As I went through the standard screening, I had to take everything out of my pockets, place them into a bowl and go through the metal detector. I also had to take my phone out and also place it in the bowl.

For years I have worn a phone clip on my belt to hold my phone. Also, since I usually try to get the largest iPhone, I have been known to be teased about how I carry my phone. During my race for Auditor someone even tweeted out, "Is Representative Harmon the only person that wears an iPad on his belt?"

At that time, one problem was that most of the clips would get locked up, especially when you took them off and tried to put them back on. When you tried to snap it back into place, they make a loud POP!

Yes, after going through the line to clear me to go in, I retrieved my things and worked to get my phone and phone clip in place, and yes it made a loud POP. The security people and everyone around flinched and looked around and I had to say, "I'm sorry, I'm sorry."

Thankfully, I did still get to go in and hear Trump speak that day. That was in addition to the speeches he made at the convention itself. He did, as always, give a great speech and solidified my belief that he would be our next President.

CHAPTER TWENTY FIVE

THE THINGS WE DO AS A CANDIDATE!

Somewhere along the line it seems like most candidates do things the average person would not do. One of those things I did not once but twice (because I wasn't smart enough to do just once) was to play in what is known as Donkey Basketball.

If you are familiar with basketball, say via watching the University of Kentucky Wildcats or your local high school team, well this isn't it. Imagine the same court, usually in an old school gym converted into a community center, but much more humorous, at least for the spectators.

Basically, a group who has donkeys brings in ten donkeys that are divided into five donkeys for each team playing. There is a wide array of personalities in these donkeys but at least one on each team is a bit wild. The key; don't get the wild one.

The rules are simple, you ride donkeys and play basketball all while having a small hat similar to a baseball batting helmet without a strap on your head as you fall. Thankfully, my good friend State Senator (formally State Representative) Jimmy Higdon did give me a bit of advice.

You only have to be on the donkey when you pass, or you shoot. As you can imagine, they didn't enforce walking too often. When you are not passing or shooting, you can get off your donkey. This helps minimize falling but does create another problem. Sometimes when you try to guide your donkey, he decides that's not the direction he wants to go. So, at times it seems like you're dragging the donkey trying to get to the ball.

Now I did play basketball through my freshman year of high school, and I use the term play loosely, but I actually did ok with donkey basketball. One of the times I played I scored the first basket.

The main thing is you wanted to score, and you wanted to come out of the event alive while minimizing how sore you were going to be the next day. It was always for a worthy cause and trust me the donkeys were fine. I don't ever recall one of them getting hurt. I can't really say the same for the humans, but we knew what we were getting into.

If you were less than enthusiastic about riding a donkey, a few politicians became the official pooper scoopers which also added humor to the event. In my two times participating I was never wise enough to play that role. Both times I played were in Mackville Kentucky and I appreciated the opportunity to help the Community Center. The gym I played in was the one my Dad had played for real on and so that was kind of neat as well.

Besides Donkey Basketball, another interesting role a politician in rural areas might be asked to participate in was Bessie Bingo. I was asked to be the judge in Bessie Bingo.

Now State Senator Dan Kelly once told me you never want to judge a baby contest or a beauty contest because you only make one person happy. Unfortunately, he never provided guidance on Bessie Bingo.

Oh, you don't know what Bessie Bingo is? Let me back up. Bessie Bingo is where they mark off a grid in a field with letters one way and numbers the other. Then they release a cow into the grid and wherever the cow poops the judge places a tobacco stick into the ground marking the specific grid. Whoever purchased that spot wins the raffle.

First, I wondered if it was rigged since I checked with the farmer who brought the cow, and her name was not Bessie. The more appropriate term would have been the generic cow pile bingo. LOL.

Anyway, the whole thing seems simple and to judge, you only have to mark the spot. Easy right? Well, no. While the crowd looks on waiting for this poor cow to poop, the judge (being me this time) also waits and follows the cow around hoping that a bathroom break is fast in coming.

But it was not! One time I waited an entire hour before I judged that a simple squirt was sufficient to deem the cow had pooped. Yes, you become the butt of jokes, but it was worth helping out for a good cause. I believe it was for the Willisburg Volunteer Fire Department.

Whether you are playing Donkey Basketball, Judging Bessie Bingo, or some other interesting event like being in a dunking booth (yes did that as well) it is always good to both help out and get to know the citizens who you represent and care about even if they don't all agree with you always.

Those are experiences I will never forget. Trust me, I couldn't if I wanted to.

Donkey Basketball

CHAPTER TWENTY SIX

FANCY FARM

One of my favorite aspects of campaigning other than meeting so many great people is the yearly trek to Fancy Farm. Although the Fancy Farm picnic is technically a fundraiser for St. Jerome Catholic Church, the main focus is political competitors coming to the stage to battle it out (verbally anyway.) There were also pre-events with Republicans the night before, and breakfast.

I remember Senator McConnell saying how when he started going to Fancy Farm, he was one of the few Republicans that were on the stage. By the time I came around in 2015 when I ran against incumbent Auditor Adam Edelen, the stage was reasonably balanced with about a 50/50 mix. At the writing of this book, it is almost all Republican.

The way the stage is set up when you as the speaker look out, Democrats are on the right and Republicans are on your left. There tends to be a lot of booing and chanting from the opposite party to the speaker and cheers from the speaker's party, so giving a 3–6-minute speech depending on how much time you are assigned can be tough. And you want to finish on time because when you don't, they run you off the stage with music.

Thankfully, the gentleman who prepared me for Fancy Farm did an excellent job. He had my wife and my mom beat on pots and pans while he played loud music and had me give my speech over the noise. It made me realize I had to shorten and rewrite my speech.

He also suggested I drink a lot of water. The day of the event, I went to McDonald's after the breakfast event and drank 6-7 large waters when their large was still large. And it did help, but I also made sure I went to the bathroom before going on stage.

Now that first year I worked so hard to memorize my speech because I wasn't going to use my notes. Then I noticed when Senator McConnell went to the stage, he pulled out a piece of crumpled up paper and read directly from it. After that, I always used notes.

My first year in 2015 was pretty standard in that I presented myself while also making fun hopefully in good humor of the other side. After that first year, my friend State Representative Jonathan Shell (now Agriculture Commissioner) came up to me and said, "You sound just like Jeff Foxworthy."

The next year, and for several other years afterward, I did a Jeff Foxworthy-like routine. But instead of, "You might be a Redneck if,," it was "You might be a Liberal Democrat if," or something similar. I also incorporated a David Letterman-type card flip after each joke which went over very well.

I'm going to include the scripts to my speeches in this book as best as I can, but really to get the best effect you need to Google or go to YouTube and search "Mike Harmon Fancy Farm 2015, 2016," etc. Hopefully, the flashbacks are still funny. And remember, the video will not match the script 100% as changes were made on the fly that day.

FANCY FARM 2015
https://youtu.be/6K6h30Who6A

Wow, what a great crowd!

It's great to be part of such a wonderful place and a fantastic Kentucky tradition.

This is my very first Fancy Farm. So let me make sure I have this straight.

These folks over here boo no matter what I say, even though deep down in their heart they know I'm going to be a much better Auditor than Adam Edelen?

(Pause and smile)

Well, that's ok, go ahead and boo, I'm a big guy. I won't cry like Jack Conway.

Now let me tell you a little bit about my opponent. If you haven't heard about him yet, don't worry. No one else has either. That's why he didn't run for governor.

I know Adam talks a lot about being born into a farm family in Meade County, but did you know Adam actually graduated from an elite prep school in Louisville? Of course, if you talk with Adam, you'd think I agreed with every decision he's made since he switched from the Young Republicans to the Young Democrats in High School in hopes of being governor someday.

I guess I understand. He is very deliberate with his words. Why, he even traveled all the way to South Carolina just so he could praise Obama, and he wouldn't even fill out his KY Right to Life Questionnaire. I just thought Adam was more about transparency. By the way, I was endorsed by the KY Right to Life

But enough about my opponent. Let's talk about the new big baby in my life.

No, I'm not talking about Jack Conway. Just because he swore to protect & defend the State Constitution, which included defending traditional marriage, broke down crying, and refused do his job, doesn't mean we should keep bringing it up, again, and again, and again.

No, I'm talking about my very first grandchild, a boy, Aiden, born a little over a month ago, weighing nine pounds 13.7 ounces at birth.

I have pictures of him on my phone. But I don't guess we have time. See me afterwards.

Now I was speaking with him just the other day, and he said, PaPaw? (He calls me PaPaw.)

"PaPaw, I got a call from a "Steve" the other day. He said something about if I maxed out to somebody named Andy something or another's campaign, he'd help me secure the State Diaper commercial contract. I didn't even know there was such a thing, but he said not to worry, his good friend Barack taught him how to do this executive thingy with a pen and a phone."

I told him, you might want to be careful with that.

I went on to tell him about my race for Auditor.

I told Aiden not to worry. I know Adam's allies in House Democrat Leadership over the last several decades have put us in a tight spot with billions in unfunded liabilities and more and more debt, but your PaPaw and the whole Republican slate will win this year and next year I'll help the Republican's in the House give my good friend Speaker Stumbo the long-awaited retirement he legislated to himself a few years ago.

For more information go to: **Mikeharmon.com**
Thanks, and God Bless,

FANCY FARM 2016

https://youtu.be/sI290-Rks88

Wow,

First let me thank everyone from both sides here at Fancy Farm. Last year was my very first Fancy Farm, and what a great welcome. This year is my first time back as your Kentucky State Auditor, and it is truly an honor to serve.

As your State Auditor, the motto we've adopted is "Follow the Data," which means we don't target anyone, nor do we give anyone a pass based on party labels. We instead keep a watchful eye on how your tax dollars are being spent.

Of course, I always considered Fancy Farm to be a friendly elbow in the stomach type of place. And with that in mind, I want to, in advance, extend my apologies to my more conservative Democrat friends and perhaps to a few of my liberal Democrat friends as well.

Those who know me, know I like to tell a few jokes along the way. Last year my good friend Rep. Shell said I sounded just like Jeff Foxworthy and with that in mind I developed this year's speech.

So, here we go:

If you think Traditional Marriage is outdated and overrated, you might be a liberal Democrat.

If you think cutting down a tree is barbaric, but what Planned Parenthood does is just peachy. . . you might be a liberal Democrat.

If you think second amendment protections apply only to elected officials and Hollywood bodyguards. . . you might be a liberal Democrat.

If you think Benghazi is something you put on a rash... you might be a liberal Democrat.

If you think climate change is the greatest threat to our nation, but that ISIS is just a JV team. . . you just might be a liberal Democrat.

If you think having a secure email server means waterproofing your basement. . . you might be a liberal Democrat.

And finally, if you can promise to put coal miners out of work and STILL expect to win coal country. . . you just might be a liberal Democrat.

All kidding aside, no matter if you are Republican, Democrat, or Independent, the liberal values of Hillary Clinton and Barack Obama have devastated Kentucky, which is no laughing matter. If you want real change for real people, then I encourage you to go to the polls in November and vote for Republican candidates from the top of the ticket to the bottom.

Thank you and God Bless.

FANCY FARM 2017

https://youtu.be/V4ylOYPnp6c

Thank you all. It's always great being in West Kentucky and especially being here at Fancy Farm. This is now my third year in a row, so I'm becoming more accustomed to the great people here and maybe a little bit of the ribbing.

It's great to see both parties represented here -- Republicans on one side, and those who are still looking for the Clerk's office to change their registration on the other side.

You know, I wish Governor Bevin was here again this year, but I suppose it's just as well. He and General Beshear might have challenged each other to a duel and that would have disqualified both from holding office. But, we're fortunate at the Auditor's office in that we get along with both of these gentlemen. Of course, it helps that General Beshear hasn't sued us.

(Turning to General Beshear): We're good, right?

As I explained last year at this event, the motto I brought to the Auditor's office is to "Follow the Data," which means we don't target anyone, nor do we give anyone a pass based on party labels. Instead, we keep a watchful eye on how your tax dollars are being spent at all levels of government. And, as much as I enjoy telling jokes, at the Auditor's office, we take this job seriously.

This is a time of bold conservative leadership in Frankfort with a new Republican majority in the House joining the majority in Senate and working with Governor Bevin and the executive branch.

It's been my honor serving as your State Auditor of Public Accounts for over a year and half now, and I am so proud of our staff as we do over 600 audits a year. This ranges from audits of large state agencies, to audits of your local county officials.

During my first year in office, we conducted the first-ever audit of the Kentucky Law Enforcement Foundation Program Fund, which receives over $60 million each year, and we made recommendations to ensure more of this money goes to support the law enforcement officers it was intended for.

We not only continued looking into the University of Louisville Foundation, but were able to complete the work and provide a road map to address the institution's governance and transparency problems for a fraction of the cost of the forensic audit that followed.

One of the most shocking things we discovered was that the multi-million-dollar Foundation couldn't produce a budget-to-actual report. Now, even my home church in Junction City has budget-to-actual reports, and I bet St. Jerome's right here has them too! At any rate, as a result of my office's recommendations, the Foundation board this year approved its first-ever line-item budget.

Also, this spring, we released a report on the Kentucky Horse Park, where we discovered widespread mismanagement of contracts. Eighty percent of food service contracts tested were not billed according to contract. Some were higher and some lower, but incredibly, documents to support modifications were routinely shredded--which made our job a little more interesting.

Recently, we audited the KFC Yum Center and pointed out that taxpayers are footing 75% of the bill for this arena. We also pointed out flaws in the original financing plan for the Arena and encouraged all those involved and especially those who benefited most from the arena to come together to assure the stability of the Yum Center going forward.

These are just a few examples of the work we've done in my administration, and going forward, we will continue to Follow the Data to protect your tax dollars and help state and local governments be more efficient, effective, and ethical.

Thank you for the opportunity to serve this great Commonwealth, thanks again for the opportunity to be here today, and Thanks and God Bless.

FANCY FARM 2018

https://youtu.be/zxAe-zunNRA

Thank you all. It's always great being in West Kentucky and especially being here at Fancy Farm. This is now my fourth year in a row, so I'm becoming even more accustomed to the great people here and hopefully the good-natured teasing.

As I have explained before, the motto I brought to the Auditor's office is to "Follow the Data," which means we don't target anyone and we don't give anyone a pass, we just simply Follow the Data.

A lot of people don't really understand the role of the State Auditor's Office – some people think we are like the IRS, but that's not the case. Instead, our role is to be "the people's auditor" holding government accountable not the taxpayers.

It's been my honor serving as your State Auditor, and I am so proud of our office. We as a team have done some very important work including just recently a historic, first ever outside examination of the Administrative Office of the Courts.

We found serious issues with their operations and their lack of policies. One example was leasing office space for a Supreme Court Justice from a company owned by his sons without a documented explanation as to why it was chosen even though it was three times higher than another option.

There's a lot more but you'll have to go to auditor.ky.gov to see.

And we are always keeping a watchful eye trying to make sure government is efficient, effective, and ethical. With that in mind, we have worked with members of the General Assembly on several pieces of legislation including SB144 sponsored by Sen. Stan Humphries, that should help many of our Sheriffs and County Clerks save 25 to 50% on their audits. Common sense solutions that save our counties money are good policies on both sides of the political aisle.

That being said, Fancy Farm wouldn't be Fancy Farm without a little bit of political humor. And this year, as a throwback to 2016, I'm bringing back an amended Jeff Foxworthy routine.

Instead of "You might be a liberal democrat," this year's theme is "you might be a Democrat looking to run for governor."
So, here we go!

If you think Democrats who were in Majority Leadership for decades aren't responsible for underfunding the pension systems, you might be a Democrat looking to run for governor!

If your name is synonymous with the future outlook of your party, you might be a Democrat looking to run for governor! (I gave you 2 Rocky, you're that important)

If you think medical marijuana has anything to do with the job of Secretary of State, you might be a Democrat looking to run for governor! (By the way, Allision, congrats on the baby, they're great but sometimes can be rebellious---probably grow up to be a Republican)

If you've ever accused me of being a martini drinking jet setter when everyone knows I'm a slow poke teetotaler, you might be a Democrat looking to run for governor!

If your grandfather was governor and you just don't understand why you haven't been, you might be a Democrat looking to run for governor!

And finally, if you've asked Siri to set a weekly reminder to sue Governor Bevin, well, you are definitely a Democrat running for governor!

Let's follow the data, since Republicans have been in the majority of both House and Senate along with the governor's office, there have been Billions more funding provided to the struggling pensions systems and to education, and billions more invested by private companies in KY.

Now is not the time to change course back to the open seas and risk forever being lost in an ocean of mediocrity. We must keep KY sailing in the right direction toward opportunity and prosperity for all Kentuckians. Thank you for the opportunity to serve this great Commonwealth, thanks again for the opportunity to be here today, and thanks and God Bless you all.

FANCY FARM 2019
https://youtu.be/THZUbL2EkGE

First, let me thank everyone- Republican, Democrat, and Independent here at Fancy Farm. If you want to know more about the great work of our Team and my campaign, go to www.mikeharmon.com.

You know when I first went into the Auditor's office, I told all our auditors we don't target anyone and we don't give anyone a pass, we simply follow the data. And I believe we have held to that principle and hope to continue our great work for another 4 years.

Now for some fun.

As you know, it's been said I sound just like Jeff Foxworthy and with that in mind this year's theme is "You might be a Far-Left Democrat." If you want to abolish ice, even in your freezer, you might be a Far-Left Democrat.

If you've ever publicly been against Trump, for Trump, and then Against Trump all before your first cup of coffee, you might be a Far-Left Democrat.

If you just ran as a Liberal and lost in Louisville but still think you can run as a Liberal statewide and win, you might be a Far-Left Democrat. If think cutting down a tree is barbaric, but what Planned Parenthood does is just peachy, you might be a Far-Left Democrat.

If your Father failed to ever fully fund the pension systems, but you want to replace a governor that has, you might be a Far-Left Democrat.

If the existence of Coal and Cow gas haunts your dreams, you might be a Far-Left Democrat.

If you've ever stumbled onto a stage and given a bizarre speech about an Arkansas Traveler, you might be a Far-Left Democrat.

If your name is Andy, but perhaps it should be a boy name Sue, and Sue, and Sue you might be a Far-Left Democrat.

If you think the Preamble to the US Constitution starts, For the people, instead of We the people, you might be a Far-Left Democrat.

If you think the Bill of Rights should be a Bill of Lefts, you might be a Far-Left Democrat.

And finally, if you are anywhere on the 2019 Democrat ticket, well, you might be a Far-Left Democrat.

You know, if you are a democrat that's pro-life, pro-second amendment, and pro USA, you might be a Democrat left behind by your party. . . but guess what, there's still plenty of room on this side . . . for you.

All kidding aside, no matter if you are Republican, Democrat, Libertarian, or Independent, the Far-Left values of the current Democrat Party have devastated Kentucky, which is no laughing matter.

With Republicans at the helm, the ship is now headed in the right direction, so let's keep on course, and make this Commonwealth the best it can be.

Please vote for me, Mike Harmon for reelection to Auditor.

Thank you and God Bless.

Fancy Farm 2019 — L-R Ty Sharp, Johnathon McQuerry, Blake Carpenter, Nick Nash, Mike (PaPaw), Michael Mingey, Daniel McQuerry, Sara Beth Gregory

Fancy Farm 2019

FANCY FARM 2021

https://youtu.be/i4SuURna5s4

It is so great to be back here at Fancy Farm after the year that we've had, and I want to first thank St. Jerome's Parish and all the organizers who've worked so hard to put on this picnic.

So. . . the last time I was here I was running for reelection, and something happened in 2019. I became the oldest currently serving Constitutional Officer not by one, not by two, but by almost ten years.

The closest is Sec. Adams. He's 45. The next closest is Governor Beshear at 43. I'll be 55 in October.

So you can imagine, being the old guy on the block, I was feeling a little down, and the other day, my wonderful wife of 31+ years, Lynn (look at Lynn) comes in and I'm looking in the mirror and she says, "What are you doing?" So, I look at her and say, look, I look so old, and I look so tired, can you say one good thing about me to make me feel good about myself.

So she looks and she thinks, and she looks, and she thinks and finally she says, "Well, at least your eyesight is still good." (Look at Lynn.)

Well, I guess if you are going to have one good thing as an Auditor it should be your eyesight.

. . . some of you may have heard. . . I made a big announcement a few weeks ago.

I imagine over the next several months, some of my friends may make similar announcements. . .

And in the spirit of my favorite modern president, Ronald Reagan, I want to make a promise. . .

"I will not make age an issue in this campaign . . . I am not going to exploit for political purposes any of my opponents' youth and inexperience."

Well, it has been a long journey. . .

After losing my first two races for the State House, I had several tell me if only I would change to Democrat, I could win.

But of course, I couldn't do that because my values line up with the Republican Party. . . Pro Life, Pro Family, Pro Second Amendment, Pro Law Enforcement.

Now I know when I come to Fancy Farm, one of things people expect are some good old fashioned "you might be a liberal Democrat" jokes, and I certainly don't like to disappoint,

You know, It's a shame the Democrats didn't come but "They'd rather be fancy In Louisville than spend time down in Fancy Farm."

All right, so here we go:

If you think requiring a photo ID to vote is outrageous but requiring a vaccine passport is AOK, "you might be a liberal Democrat"

If you think funding Mask Enforcement is more important than funding Law Enforcement, "you might be a liberal Democrat"

If Taco Bell is the closest you want to get to the Mexican border, "you might be a liberal Democrat"

If you think people attending church are criminals, but abortion clinics are essential, "you might be a liberal Democrat"

If the biggest crowd you saw last year was the line of unemployment applicants outside your office, "you might be a liberal Democrat"

Really though, I know even our liberal Democrat friends actually just want to help people. . . well, those that cut their hair anyway.

And one I thought I could retire after the 2019 elections, but apparently not,

If your name is Andy, but it should be a boy named Sue, and Sue, and Sue, then you just might be a liberal Democrat.

In 2023, the voters of Ky will have a chance to help Andy Beshear in the same way his policies helped many of them — by sending him home!

The liberal policies and government overreach we see coming from the White House and the Governor's Mansion might be well intentioned, but those policies have also closed businesses, created record levels of unemployment, and kept a lot of kids from getting the education they deserve.

If you're a Democrat here at FF today, your party leaders have quite literally abandoned you.

Especially if you are a Democrat who's pro-life, pro-second amendment, and pro USA, you might be a Democrat left behind by your party. . . but guess what, there's still plenty of room on this side for you.

Please consider coming to this side. This is where the people who care about protecting your liberties, your faith, and your ability to take care of your family stand.

Thank you and God Bless.

FANCY FARM 2022
https://youtu.be/LYVeEqUrnXM

It is great to be back here at Fancy Farm. I want to thank everyone at St. Jerome's Parish who works so hard to put on this event.

First, I want to say that I and all of Kentucky have the people of Eastern and Southeastern KY in our prayers after the most recent flooding.

Also, I appreciate the strong spirit of the people of this area, and please know that you remain in my prayers, and the prayers of many across the Commonwealth, after the devastation of the tornadoes that hit especially hard right here in Graves County.

I am honored to be in my seventh year serving as your KY State Auditor, and I've made it a point to attend the Fancy Farm picnic every year I've been invited.

That's just one of the differences between me and the current Governor.

Now, last year, I thought the Governor didn't want to be the only Democrat on stage, but this year he chose not to come for what I can only imagine is to avoid being on stage with Charles Booker.

I do want to give Charles Booker credit for showing up to represent the Democrat Party here at Fancy Farm.

There aren't many people left in Kentucky who want to defend the woke and broke liberal agenda of the current Democrat Party.
Now, for some reason, it seems like Governor Beshear is afraid to come back to Fancy Farm.

I guess that shouldn't be a surprise because he's let fear drive most of his policy decisions –

he shut down businesses so people couldn't work,

he shut down church buildings so people couldn't worship,

and he even shut down the road that goes between the State Capitol and the annex building -- all because of fear.

I don't know about you, but I've had enough of government making decisions that are motivated by fear.

That's why I'm running for governor and traveling around the state to share my message of choosing freedom over fear.

Now I was the first Republican to announce a run for governor, but the field is getting pretty crowded. Just like people complaining about Beshear/Biden inflation, everyone is doing it.

I want to get back to a time where the economy is growing, people have good jobs, kids are getting a good education in an actual classroom, and opportunity is available to everyone.

Now, one of my favorite things about Fancy Farm is that joke-telling is encouraged, even if they are "Dad-jokes" or in my case "Grand-dad jokes."

The theme for this year is "You Might Be a Beshear/Biden Democrat/!" All right, are we ready?

1) If you tell everybody the economy is on fire, but fail to say it's a dumpster fire You might be a Beshear/Biden Democrat.

2) If you believe "man" dates are great, but you just wish they could be called "person" dates,

You might be a Beshear/Biden Democrat
3) If you think concerned parents should be prosecuted as domestic terrorist, but shoplifters should be praised as savvy shoppers

You might be a Beshear/Biden Democrat

4) If you're releasing oil from the strategic reserves to lower gas prices. . . in China,

You might be a Beshear/Biden Democrat.

5) If you believe the Constitution provides a right to an abortion, but not a right to keep and bear arms,

You might be a Beshear/Biden Democrat

(And you might want to re-read the Constitution)

6) If you've ever responded to a jeopardy question of ways to improve safety with, "What is defund the police."

You might be a Beshear/Biden Democrat

And lastly, if you're a governor who refuses to show up to the super bowl of Kentucky politics two years in a row

Well, you might be a Beshear going home in 2023.

One thing that's for sure, is the voters of KY will have a clear choice in 2023, and I hope you'll choose freedom at MikeHarmon.com

Thank you and God Bless.

FANCY FARM 2023

https://youtu.be/k1UoqMYiDC4

It is great to be back here at Fancy Farm. I want to thank everyone at St. Jerome's Parish who works so hard to put on this event.

I am honored to be in my eighth year serving as your KY State Auditor, and I've made it a point to attend the Fancy Farm picnic every year I've been invited.

Sadly, this will be my last year as Auditor, but I want to thank each & every one of you here and in KY who have given me the honor to stand before you on this stage and to serve this great Commonwealth.

Now, one of my favorite things about Fancy Farm is joke-telling, even if they are "Dad-jokes" or in my case "Grand-dad jokes."

This year's theme is "You Might Be a Beshear/Biden Democrat."

All right, are we ready?

7) If you think sin is abhorrent, but the only thing that is a sin is voting Republican, You might be a Beshear/Biden Democrat.

8) If you've ever called someone a science denier, . . . but then can't define what a woman is,

You might be a Beshear/Biden Democrat.

9) If the only Hunter you think should have a gun is Hunter Biden, you might be a Beshear/Biden Democrat,

10) If you think shutting down a church will save a life, but shutting down an abortion clinic ehh? You might be a Beshear/Biden Democrat.

11) If your idea of good public policy is taking credit for other people's work. . . you might be a Beshear/Biden Democrat.

12) If you want to sell a combined pack of Mr. and Mrs. Potato Head parts, and call the toy Gender Neutral Potato Head,

You might be a Beshear/Biden Democrat.

13) "If you think communicating with the General Assembly is putting their number on a Do Not Call list. . . you might be a Beshear/Biden Democrat."

14) And finally (and sadly. . . if you've ever vetoed a bill protecting children from mutilation and teachers from being bullied by an Education Commissioner, you are definitely a Beshear/Biden Democrat.

As I close, please don't be deceived. The only party that wants to protect your children's innocence, protect your safety, and protect your KY Family values is the Republican Party, and I look forward to our next Governor Daniel Cameron and the entire Republican slate, defending the beliefs that Kentuckians hold dear.

Thank you and God Bless.

Nothin Fancy Farm Mike (PaPaw)

Nothin Fancy Farm L-R Lt. Gov Jenean Hampton, Mike (PaPaw),
Mike Maggard, Michael Johnson

CHAPTER TWENTY SEVEN

NOTHIN' FANCY FARM

I would be amiss after mentioning Fancy Farm if I failed to mention Nothin' Fancy Farm. This event in many ways was set up as a counter to Fancy Farm. It was started primarily by two of my friends, Mike Maggard and Sally Oh.

Nothin' Fancy Farm was held on Mike's farm and was intended to allow everyone, not just politicians, to have three minutes to speak their mind. It also tended to be much more Liberty minded.

In reality, I have been going to Nothin' Fancy Farm longer than Fancy Farm. The very first year I went to was either 2010 or 2011 but it was during Phil and I's race for governor/lt. governor. I don't think I've missed one I have been invited to since that time.

After the speaking, they tried to have music the rest of the day. Also, there was a potluck prior to the speaking.

Over the years, Mike became a dear friend of mine. During my race for governor, he even made his own "Harmon for Governor" sign on a tarp that he pulled up on his barn, and he even wrote a song about my campaign.

Mike, Sally, and those who attended were and are a great group of people who believe in our country and the freedoms it should never surrender.

CHAPTER TWENTY EIGHT

BONUS JOKE FROM MY MOM!

Now throughout this book I have tried to weave in jokes I have told on the trail and if I miss any, I'll try to include a separate list towards the end, but I did want to include one my Mom told me recently that I haven't had a chance to use a lot since I'm no longer on the trail.

There was this old man who was backing out of a parking lot when he just barely taps a man in an expensive vehicle, a Mercedes I believe. The old man gets out and the man in the expensive car jumps out quickly and starts yelling at the old gentleman.

"You hit my car!! You are going to give me $10,000 right now or I'm going to beat you up!"

The old man was a bit nervous and uncertain what to do so he said, "Please let me call my son. He'll know what to do. He trains dolphins.

So, the old man calls his son and tells him what happened and that this guy was going to beat him up if he didn't come up with the money.

The old man gets off the phone and says his son who trains dolphins is on the way and he can take care of the situation.

The son arrives quickly, gets out of the car, and beats up the man who was threatening his Father.

The son then goes over to his Dad and says, "You OK?" After seeing his Dad is OK, he then says to his Dad, "Dad, I wish you would quit telling people I train dolphins. I train Seals."

CHAPTER TWENTY NINE

PHILOSOPHIES ON LEADERSHIP

After being elected to Auditor in 2015, NASACT (National Association of State Auditors, Comptrollers and Treasurers) asked me to submit a chapter on leadership to be used in a book that they handed out to new officials. Although not identical to what I submitted to them, I have included some of the same concepts for your review.

The first thing I would say is to recruit exceptional people. The one thing I've noticed about good leaders over the years is that they start with recruitment. Former University of Kentucky basketball coach John Calipari had been criticized over the years because of his "One and Done" recruitment techniques, but no one can argue with his success especially in the first ten years.

Year after year, he continued to take teams into the NCAA tournament and usually went very deep into the field. He is a great coach and I've still seen him take teams of lesser raw talent deep into the tournament, but he always recruits the very best, teaches them well, gives them some freedom, and then pushes them to be their absolute best.

I certainly don't want to try and compare myself to such a successful individual as Coach Cal, but I believe I was successful in implementing some of those same techniques at the Auditor's office. It was my goal to recruit exceptional people, people better than me, more qualified than me, and provide them with the direction and vision I had for the office.

Given my eight years as Auditor, I could certainly list many individuals who fit that category and almost all who I considered to be like family. However, I will briefly mention two, both of whom started out as my general counsel at different times and eventually became my chief of staff. Both also I consider dear friends and appreciate their expertise and wisdom they brought to the office.

The first was Sara Beth Gregory. She started as my first general counsel. I had served with Sara Beth in the House before she went onto the State Senate. After my victory as Auditor in 2015, I had intended to reach out and see if she would be willing to be part of my team. But before I could even call, I had multiple members from the State Senate call and let me know it would be a good idea for me to make her a part of my administration.

Of course, I did make her a part of my team and she served as general counsel for almost a year when my first chief of staff came in and let me know she had accepted another position with the new Speaker. So, I didn't miss a beat. My current chief of staff called Sara Beth in, and we asked her to sit down.

I looked at Sara Beth and said, Ginger is leaving so you are getting a field promotion and will now be my new chief of staff. Although she was stunned momentarily, she quickly got to work, and we began the process of building an adjusted team including a new general counsel.

Sara Beth served on my team for a total of seven years before she ran for and won the position of a circuit judge in her hometown.

The second individual I will comment on is Jon Grate. After Governor Bevin's loss in the 2019 Election, Jon was on what we sadly joked about being on a sinking ship. At that time Jon was serving in the Justice and Public Safety Cabinet.

Since our general counsel (not Sara Beth) had just left and we needed a new one, we jokingly said we airlifted Jon off the sinking ship. Prior to serving as a Deputy Secretary and Acting Secretary, Jon had also been a bill drafter in the General Assembly and he had helped draft some of my bills and amendments.

Jon served on my team well for several years until he retired -- we thought that was the last time we would see Jon during my term. However, after he retired, we had a staffer leave and after Jon had been out the mandatory time for retirement, I asked if he would be willing to come back and he agreed but in a different position.

A few months after he came back, Sara Beth won her election for circuit judge and so I was in need of a new chief of staff. I offered and he accepted, and he served out the remainder of my term.

Both of these individuals were smarter and better than me and their expertise contributed greatly to my success as Auditor. And as mentioned, both are dear friends that I am so grateful to have gotten to know during my two terms.

A third individual that fits these criteria but who was with me a little under a year was my first chief of staff, Ginger Hughes Kelly. She had a great amount of experience in distinct aspects of government and served my team well for almost one year when a new opportunity presented itself to her. Towards the end of my first year, she was offered the position of chief of staff for the new Speaker of the House in Kentucky.

The new Speaker's party had gone from minority to super majority overnight and needed someone who had experience in multiple areas of government and personnel to help guide the new Speaker.

I told her, "Well, I guess I am just like John Calipari. I recruit the absolute best and they're 'one and done.'" But in all sincerity, it is important to recruit and hire people better than your own abilities and knowledge. I want people smarter than I am around me.

That's not to slight myself. I graduated high school with a 4.0 (when 4.0 was the highest you could get) and was valedictorian of my class. I went on to graduate college with a 3.83 and a triple major in Math, Statistics, and Theater (I always joke that way I know the Math and I know the Stats and what I don't know I can act like I know.) However, if the only people you put around yourself are those who are of equal or lesser abilities, then you are placing a cap on how well you succeed.

Finally, on this issue, do all you can to help people grow and become the best employee, the best individual, and the best person possible. You will lose some, perhaps many, to other employers, but you might be surprised how many stay and how many want to come back. And even if they don't, you just might find out they are promoting your office to the next young superstar because you actually care about people and their goals and their visions.

John Calipari would never want to hold back a player from making it to the next level, and although I'm no Coach Cal, I wouldn't either.

Another quality that I think some leaders forget is that you don't always have to reinvent the wheel. I can think of two specific times in my life (I'm sure there are more) where I had to realize you can't and shouldn't always try to completely start from scratch. You could, in fact, build on the foundation of those who preceded you.

The first was when I worked at Trim Masters, which was an auto parts manufacturer in Harrodsburg, KY. At that time, we primarily made seat covers that would be used in cars manufactured by Toyota.

Now, I had worked briefly on the floor of the plant in assembly, (and much to the excitement of myself as well as probably my group leader) I ended up applying for and was promoted to a position in Production Control. I served in that capacity for about a year when I was asked to go to second shift as an assistant manager. At the same time, they hired a second assistant manager for the second shift as well. In addition, they had a manager for this shift who had not been there long.

Unfortunately, the manager was dealing with personal problems. As a result, the assistants received little training or guidance. Don't get me wrong. I enjoyed the feeling of a field commander coming in every night, seeing where we were short on troops (well, employees), having to rebalance lines, and shift individuals in order to meet our production goals with people less trained than day shift.

Every night, you knew by the end of the night whether you had won or lost the battle. We had about 350 employees with at least fifty out on most nights and as many as one hundred out on many a Friday.

It was not uncommon to deal with employees fighting among themselves over various issues as if we had returned to high school. And inevitably, it seemed like we had the rescue squad out almost every Friday for one reason or another.

So, to say that this environment was stressful would be an understatement. Even in this environment, I made a lot of new friends who I cherish today, but it was tough, especially without much training.

Thankfully, I befriended a guy in Quality Control who helped provide me with some guidance as well as friends I had on first shift who I knew because I had been in Production Control. However, I did have to develop what I jokingly called the "Harmon Method of Management."

Scenario: Someone runs up to you and says, "Mike, we have this huge problem."

Me: "So what is it?"

They describe the problem and then I asked the following:

Me: "Has this ever happened before?"

Them: "Yes it has!"

Me: "What did we do?"

They describe the previously offered solution.

Me: "Well, did that work?"

Them: "Uh, yes."

Me: "Well, let's do that then."

Now obviously, that didn't work in every case, but you might be surprised how often it did. There is always room for improvement, but I've found that many times people know what to do, but they don't have enough confidence in themselves to do it.

In addition, some people are just trying to set up a scenario where they don't get blamed for a problem. I've found that the best way to deal with this is to praise when a team does something well and try to take either shared or all the blame when they fail.

That's not to say you shouldn't do a fair and honest assessment of someone's work, especially in a bureaucratic environment where that's the only way you have to judge who moves up, who stays, and who needs to go.

And you want people to know how to improve. If the feedback you are providing is constructive and not destructive, then you may have found that fine line between praise and prodding.

The second specific time I'm glad we didn't reinvent the wheel was when I came into the Auditor's office in January of 2016. I know each state is a little different in how they choose their auditor as well as the authority the Auditor has regarding staffing.

In Kentucky, the Auditor is a statewide elected position, and you run as a partisan. When taking office, you basically have two types of employees: non-merit employees, who serve at the discretion of the elected official, and merit employees, who have additional levels of protection to avoid political influence in hiring, managing, and firing of an employee.

Merit employees tend to be the rank and file, long-term employees, who do the day-to-day heavy lifting and generally make up the majority of any agency's workforce.

Non-merit employees tend to be political appointees but are still important to the overall direction and management of an agency.

As is to be expected, when I took office, we did not retain the majority of the previous administration's non-merit employees. Any newly elected official wants his or her own people in key positions, so this was not a surprise.

However, one thing I did do, was retain a few key people from the previous administration either in their same or similar positions. These were individuals who, yes, were appointments from a previous administration of the opposite party as myself, but who had also been with the agency for numerous years both in merit and non-merit positions.

After conversations with these specific individuals, it was quite obvious they were devoted to the agency and not just one previous auditor. They still maintained a fondness for the individual that provided them with an opportunity, but they were devoted to the success of the agency.

That decision, one made not just by myself, but by a transition team I had put into place, turned out to be a particularly good one. We faced multiple challenges when I took office, and the experience and continuity of these retained individuals was invaluable.

Just think of my first example.

"Have we faced this challenge before?"

"Yes."

"What did we do?"

"Did that work?"

"Let's do that again."

Now obviously I had a specific direction I wanted to see the office go, but so much of what we did is the same year after year. I describe it as the ship is already built, all we are doing is changing the rudder (and hopefully not running the ship into an iceberg.)

So, whether it is dealing with county audits, state audits, personnel issues, or budget issues, that knowledge was extremely helpful. My advice to you is if you are taking over from a previous administration, don't feel like you have to eliminate every single "at will" employee.

I would carefully review who is there currently, see who has the experience and devotion at the agency, and then select the best individuals to retain.

Another lesson I learned over the years was that failure can provide focus. I've always said you learn a whole lot more from failure than you do from success. Of course, success is a lot sweeter, but failure, when you don't let it keep you from getting back up, and you're willing to do the "postmortem," can provide a new-found focus.

As was mentioned earlier in this book, in 1996 after I went down to vote and realized that only one person was on the ballot for State Representative,

I thought to myself that this is not Russia. People deserve to have a choice in their elected officials, even if that vote is not cast for you.

After prayerful consideration, I decided to run in the following election in 1998. As it turned out, the previous State Representative who went unchallenged in 1996 and who had been there over twenty years, chose not to run.

However, there were three individuals of the same party running for the spot, and I was the only person of my party (an extreme minority party in the district) running for the office. After the other side's primary, I ended up running against the mayor of the largest city in the district. I raised about $3,300, compared to the other candidate, who raised $30,000 to $40,000.

I tried to speak with everyone in the district, but as you can imagine, I lost. However, with little or no money, and much to the surprise of many, I was able to claim about forty-three percent of the vote when my party only represented a little more than twenty-five percent of the registered voters of the district.

Of course, I was disappointed even though the outcome was expected. I took a little time and prayed about what happened and decided that I would make another attempt in 2000.

After reviewing the stats from the 1998 race and giving some consideration to what I could do better, I developed my adjusted plan.

I filed to run in 2000, and it ended up being a rematch of the 1998 general election. This time, I raised about $5,500, and my opponent, now the incumbent, raised somewhere around $40 to $45 thousand.

During this process, I repeated what worked previously, and then made changes in areas I felt either didn't work or could be improved upon. This time I took the ball a bit further down the field.

I went from about 43% of the vote to 49.3% of the vote and lost by a little under 200 votes. Needless to say, to get that close and fall short can be a bit painful. However, I once again took time to reflect and pray about the race and decided that I would give it one additional try.

This time, as it turned out, the gentleman I had run against in the general election twice before chose not to run again. This time, the other party had no primary but ran a local attorney in hopes of maintaining this seat for their side.

Fortunately for me, and I say this with a bit of humor, the attorney they ran had sued several local doctors and so this time I raised $30 to $35 thousand. Of course, my opponent still raised a great deal of money, about $40 to $45 thousand, and I was still a member of the minority party for the district.

But, this time, I had learned from my two failed attempts, I had maintained relationships developed from previous campaigns and had made additional adjustments from two prior failed attempts. In this particular case, I was victorious and received almost 57% of the vote.

In addition, I was the first person from my county and my political affiliation who had won this seat in 102 years. Of course, defeat comes on many levels and the higher you go, the more failures you face as you make adjustments for that next level.

Case in point, after serving in the State House for nine years, I was asked to run as the lieutenant governor candidate on a gubernatorial slate that was not only severely underfunded for a statewide race, but also was going up against two other opponents in the primary, with one pair being the sitting State Senate President and a very popular Agricultural Commissioner (and former UK Basketball Star).

Once again, we ran a strong race with little money but a lot of effort and crisscrossed the state speaking to whoever would hear us. In many cases, at events held by our party, my running mate and I would be excluded or given a small amount of time to speak in comparison to the other major slate (who in many cases would be keynote speakers with unlimited time at these events).

If it's not apparent yet, let me assure you that even with nine years of legislative service, we were not the establishment candidates, or the ones favored by our own party. As it turned out, to be outspent 15 to 1 or more and in a three-way race, we did okay. We received about 38% of the vote, compared to the winning ticket, who received 48%.

There were many who took note as to what a great race we ran, but to quote an old movie, "If you ain't first, you're last." I even later (after the team who beat us lost that fall to the incumbent) had a staffer from the then-current sitting governor who told me they were sweating bullets the night of our primary as they had numbers that showed we had a strong chance of winning in the fall had we cleared that race.

However, it was a wonderful experience, and I met a great bunch of people throughout the state, making new friends, and creating a network that at the time I didn't realize how helpful they would be in the future. I did as usual do a "postmortem" on the race for future reference.

As it turned out, that opportunity came sooner than I imagined. As the 2015 statewide races approached, I felt a tug on my heart to make another statewide race. My initial thought was for Secretary of State as I had multiple years of experience on the Elections, Constitutional Amendments, and Intergovernmental Affairs committee.

However, after prayerful consideration, I decided not to pursue that avenue. After a series of other events and more prayerful consideration, I decided to take on a sitting incumbent who was not only a rising star in the opposite political party, but who also was expected to run against our Junior Senator after an assumed re-election victory to his current position.

The race I chose was for Auditor of Public Accounts. As discussed earlier, I do have a bit of a "Don Quixote" complex, taking on challenges no one else wants, and seemingly impossible tasks as viewed through the lens of the world.

Once again, my main weakness showed through, and my fundraising skills seemed to be my demise. I was only able to raise about $40 to $45 thousand as compared to my opponent who was the incumbent, who raised over $800 thousand. If memory serves me well, he had two super PACS assisting him.

This truly was a "David and Goliath" scenario. Although I won't go into the full story again, I was blessed on many levels. I had maintained a network from the failed 2011 race, and I had previously taken the time to honestly analyze shortcomings from the past race. Of course this was comparing a Primary to a General, but many of the same rules applied.

There is an old saying that success is when preparedness meets opportunity and, in this case, it held true. Although I continued to fail in the area of fundraising, I had learned to compensate for that weakness via "hand-to-hand combat" or in simple terms, I drove all over the state and spoke with whoever would listen to me.

I once said I would travel two hours to speak with two people, and in many cases, I did. In addition, the environment for my political party had become much more favorable, and I am certain that played a major role. But if I hadn't learned, hadn't made adjustments, hadn't continued to do what I knew had worked, even though the opportunity was there, success would not have been found.

And, yes, I did win that race, stunning many. My comments are not intended to be a pat on the back to myself. It's only intended to relate an incredible journey God allowed me to be a part of in my life.

I think sports and politics are always very good examples for other aspects of our life. When I speak to a group of kids and relate some of this story to them, I will say, "Ok, anybody here play sports?"

Usually, a large group will say, "Yes." Then I ask them, "Did you quit when you lost your first game?" Of course, they all say "No." I go on to tell them, they have great opportunities in life awaiting them if only they don't let a temporary setback or failure keep them down.

Leadership is much like that. Let's face it. No one (including myself or you) has all the answers. You will fail. How you respond to that failure will greatly determine the strength of your character and the potential success you may have in the future.

Failure can provide focus when you let it. I always like the analogy in 1 Corinthians 12, which speaks to the fact that we all have different gifts or talents. We can't all be the same thing.

Deeper into the chapter, there is an almost humorously described conversation between various body parts. Greatly paraphrasing, the eye might say, "I'm not part of the body." Or the ear says, "I'm not part of the body."

If all you have are eyes, who will hear? If all you have is ears, who will smell? The body is made up of many parts, but each part plays a vital role. If they could in fact actually have specific feelings including jealousy and envy, how difficult would that be to manage? If the eyes said, "I'm out of here!" How would we see? And so on.

Organizations, whether public or private, tend to be much like a body. They are made up of various parts (people of different talents) who all play a vital role. As leaders, we cannot take anyone, including the person some in an organization might think plays only a small role, for granted.

If you think their role is insignificant, just wait until a day, or two, or five, when they are off sick unexpectedly. You may rethink your assessment. The point being, each person on a team, if functioning properly, plays a specific role in the health of any organization.

Have you ever noticed sports teams that succeed generally play well together? I've seen teams who have one or two superstars but fail to play well together because the stars think they are the team. (This is where we usually say, there's no "I" in team).

We must, as leaders, do our best to make each member of our team feel important and relevant. We need to make sure they are receiving the proper training, the proper guidance, and the proper encouragement regardless of whether entry-level or at the top.

In addition, we need to cross-train. If you only have one eye, and it gets injured, it's hard to see. If you only have one kidney, and it stops functioning, life can begin to decline quickly.

While at Trim Masters, we always made significant efforts to cross-train. This served quite a few purposes. Obviously, if someone were out, it made it easier to balance the line, but also if you had multiple people trained in various tasks (and in this case repetitive tasks), you would rotate everyone to help reduce injury from prolonged repetition.

In any organization, if you have multiple individuals who can do different tasks, it becomes a little easier to smooth the workload and hopefully reduce turnover, which in turn reduces stress to the group. So just remember, not everyone can be an eye.

The following are some of my final thoughts I included in the chapter submitted to NASACT.

I suppose books on leadership and management have a lot in common with books on how to raise a child. First, everyone wants to write one, and second, for some reason leaders and parents can't get their employees or children to read them to know their part.

Everyone is a little different whether it be from a management standpoint or from the point of view of an employee. Don't feel like any one writer has the answers, because they don't.

Take time to review various styles and see what works for you. In the end, most people want to be appreciated, want to feel like they add value, and want to know that you care.

If you believe in what you're doing and treat people with respect and guidance, you just might be surprised that most will eventually believe as well. May you have life and have it abundantly.

CHAPTER THIRTY

I DON'T WANT A SINGLE-PAYER SYSTEM BUT. . .

I have often said I don't want a single-payer system, and that sentiment still has not changed. However, if you look at Medicare, Medicaid, Tricare, VA Hospitals, etc., you find that although some of these are earned and some are given, they still provide a government run medical system and at times do have problems (as anything run by the government.)

If you are going to have numerous different government run medical systems and/or paths to insure the population, then at least design a more efficient version and collapse all or most into one system. If I were going to suggest such a system, I would probably build on the foundation of Medicare.

Medicare, as I understand it currently, is primarily for retirees who have paid into the system for years and thereby have earned the benefits. In addition, there are many people who have been declared disabled who after being disabled for six months or more can apply to get on Medicare.

For most, Medicare is insufficient to cover the full medical cost. So typically, people will either purchase a Medicare supplement or utilize a Medicare Advantage Plan that will manage the benefit use and provide low or no cost deductibles for the user.

Medicaid is provided to individuals in financial need who cannot afford insurance and who meet certain income and asset eligibility criteria. Medicaid also can only be used at providers that agree to take and agree to the dollar amount provided for services even though it may be much lower than normally charged rates or what they agree to take from private insurance companies. So, at times you may have a Medicaid desert where there are insufficient providers who agree to the payments for the individuals to have the needed services.

In addition to the concerns already listed, there are individuals who become trapped in the Welfare cage. The benefits they receive, especially Medicaid, can be lost just by crossing a financial threshold even if that threshold is insufficient to provide equal or better coverage than what they receive from the government. This creates a strong impediment from reaching to achieve as high as they can, for fear they will not be able to provide for their family.

My suggestion would be to create a separate path within Medicare utilizing the same networks and the same pay system but also have people pay a percentage of their income above poverty to participate in the system. You would want to set the percentage rate in such a way that it would not only be actuarily sound but also at a certain point be more advantages to switch to private insurance or employer insurance. In this way you would hope to minimize the Welfare trap.

Of course, in creating this you would eliminate the need for Medicaid as anyone under the poverty level would receive free Medicare insurance. You could then shut down Medicaid and take any monies not needed to shore up the new Medicare system and block grant the differences to the states to utilize for Medicare Supplements and/or Medicare Advantage programs.

In addition, you could provide these same Medicare benefits to Veterans who could use them anywhere or use at current VA hospitals with the VA hospitals acting more as a straight provider as opposed to a captive provider. That way if VA can get to you timely then great, but if not, then a veteran can take to any willing provider.

As I said, I'm not interested in a single payer-system, but if we can create efficiencies in the current systems and begin to remove the shackles of fear of losing benefits, then we can provide a greater incentive for every American to reach for and hopefully achieve to their highest level.

CHAPTER THIRTY ONE

A CURIOUS MONKEY AND OVERREACHING GOVERNMENT

If I had to pinpoint the first time I personally dealt with government interference into my personal and business life, I would have to say it was in second grade. My teacher, Mrs. Proctor (one of 3 Mrs. Proctors at my school), interjected herself into a business transaction I had at school.

Every so often, we would be given the opportunity to order books from an order list, but we had to pay for them. My family at the time was wonderful but would have been considered financially in the lower middle class so extra money to buy books did not come easily.

As it turned out, there was a specific book, "Curious George," that I wanted but I did not have the quarter needed to purchase. Yes, it was a quarter. I'm old and I've seen what inflation can do over the decades.

I did have, however, a lunch that I brought with me to school every day. It would generally consist of a sandwich of some type (maybe bologna and Miracle Whip), a bag of chips, and a snack (Little Debbie or something similar.) On the day the order form came out and I determined I so needed this book I devised a plan.

During lunch, I offered to sell my bag of Fritos to Mary Ann Brown for the quarter I needed for the book. She, having a quarter, the very quarter I needed, agreed to the transaction and we both got what we wanted. She received a bag of chips she wanted, and I received the quarter I needed for my next transaction. (Capitalism at its finest!)

After receiving the quarter, I filled out my form and turned it in to Mrs. Proctor with the necessary funds and so all was right with the world or so I thought. Somewhere after receiving my money and spending my money, Mrs. Proctor found out about the transaction and demanded I return all or part of the money I had received from Mary Ann.

It was just like the government to demand that you return a portion or all of your profit after they have spent your money. The conversation went something like this:

Mrs. Proctor: "Mike, you cannot sell your Fritos for a quarter. You can buy that same bag of chips for ten cents anywhere else."

Me: (Knowing the value of supply and demand even in the second grade.) "Well, you can't buy them here for ten cents."

Needless to say, she was not happy with my response. Now, I was unable to return the quarter or even a portion of the quarter because she had already spent my money and was not going to return it. Also, in the second grade, they wouldn't let me file bankruptcy on this false debt forced on me by an out-of-control government.

So, I did what anyone else backed into such a corner would do, I renegotiated the deal with Mary Ann. This of course was pretty easy given she was happy with the original deal prior to this interference. I agreed that for the next two days I would give her whatever my chips for those days ended up being and she accepted this new arrangement. As it turned out, the next two days were pretzels, and given I'm not a big fan of pretzels, it worked out well for me also.

It is interesting that I had this first experience with government in-terference at such a young age, but this was one of many experiences over the years that led me to believe that government is best when it is the least. We cannot allow government to go unchecked or it becomes the monster that it is now. Much like trying to get a cow back in the barn after a door has been left open, we must be vigilant to first constrain the government and then work to reduce the government.

CHAPTER THIRTY TWO

SUFFER THE LITTLE CHILDREN

Preserving innocent unborn life was really the main reason I became interested in politics. I could never fully understand how someone could rationalize taking the life of an unborn child but perhaps it was best said when someone told me they use "rational" "lies."

In Matthew 19:14 KJV: "But Jesus said, 'Suffer little children, and forbid them not, to come unto me: for of such is the kingdom of heaven.'"

In Matthew 18:4-6 KJV "Whosoever therefore shall humble himself as this little child, the same is greatest in the kingdom of heaven. And whoso shall receive one such little child in my name receiveth me. But whoso shall offend one of these little ones which believe in me, it were better for him that a millstone were hanged about his neck, and that he were drowned in the depth of the sea."

In Jeremiah 1:5 "Before I formed thee in the belly I knew thee; and before thou camest forth out of the womb I sanctified thee, and I ordained thee a prophet unto the nations."

Certainly, it is evident that much of what I believe regarding an innocent unborn life was shaped by my faith and my personal relationship with my Lord and Savior, Jesus Christ. However, given two of my three majors in college were Math and Statistics, I also believe myself to be a man of science.

As a man of science, it is quite evident with current and past ultrasound technology that what exist in a mother's womb is more than just a lump of tissue. The ability to see so many signs of life (and a unique life at that) at very early stages of development including heart beats, movement, and even sucking a thumb should leave anyone except science deniers with the profound realization that what we see is life and to intentionally destroy such a life is nothing short of murder.

But when Satan roams the earth, he can deceive men and women of science including even some who claim to be people of faith. Though I might disagree with those who say, "You can't embrace your faith or even let it guide you in government," I find it interesting that those same people who say science is the only path allowed disavow that path when it does not fit a political narrative.

During my time in the Kentucky General Assembly, I was always in the minority so sadly we only passed one bill that would be considered a prolife bill while I was there. That bill was known as the Fetal Homicide Bill which recognized that an unborn child (at least at viability) was in fact a unique individual and if someone committed a crime against a mother that resulted in the death of her child, they would be prosecuted under the same laws that protected a child or adult.

It was not easy getting this bill passed. Democrat Leadership would not allow the bill to come to a vote primarily because it would recognize the uniqueness of an unborn child and they would have a hard time explaining how if the mother wanted her unborn child, it existed and if she didn't want her unborn child, it was just a piece of tissue.

As I understand, Republicans had been trying to pass this bill for several years and even before I arrived at the KY House. But finally, after much effort, and the frustration of many more conservative Democrats, we were able to get not only most Republicans, but also 25 Democrats to sign a Discharge Petition.

Now the one thing Democrat Leadership did not want was for their authority to be questioned. However, when it looked like they might lose to their own members, they did allow an amended version of the bill which included that the child had to be at a viable state to be voted on the floor. As you can imagine, the bill did pass by a large margin. It was odd that the bill was fought for so long but when it came to a vote most voted in favor. Politics can be funny most of the time.

Over the years, my wife also has sat on our local Pregnancy Resource Center (PRC) board two separate times. It was and is a passion of hers as well. Interestingly enough, my wife also opened my eyes to other aspects of PRCs that I had not considered and some I initially had a hard time accepting.

Of course, I knew that they worked with young ladies who were in a crisis pregnancy to see all the alternatives and not just the abortion option pushed by the other side. I also knew they shared the Gospel with these mothers to help them make the best-informed decision they could. I even knew they worked with the fathers as well.

What I had not considered early on was they also provided post abortive counseling for those who had made the decision to terminate their pregnancy. I must admit, as determined as I was to save as many unborn children as I could, I had not fully intellectually or spiritually considered the long-lasting damage done to a woman who made the decision to intentionally terminate their pregnancy.

As was explained to me primarily by my wife, the goal of PRCs are to fully love the mother and fully love the child. If the mother chooses or has chosen in the past to terminate a pregnancy, they want to still be there for them. She said they had spoken to individuals who were ten, fifteen, and even twenty years post abortive, still struggling with the ramifications of their decisions.

It is important for people to know that God's love does not end at the door of the abortion clinic. God's forgiveness, His healing, and His willingness to cleanse us and make us new if only we accept Him is there up until we take our last breath. There is peace in accepting His Grace. And there is nothing in this world that will keep Him from us except rejecting Him.

I do understand abortion can be a tough subject for a lot of people, and the lines have been drawn. I also understand if statistics are correct, there could be as many as one-third of the women in your church who have had an abortion sometime during their lives. But it is important that we continue to stand up for the truth while doing it in love for all.

Unfortunately, today's politics have tried to describe someone like me as an extremist while at the same time not confessing to their own extreme views. One such example is Kentucky Governor Andy Beshear.

His policies on life are as radical as most Democrats in leadership. During the last governor's debate with Daniel Cameron, Governor Beshear, despite saying he was not for late term abortions, was unable to say what he would consider to be the latest date a baby should be terminated even if you excluded those that took place to protect the life of the mother.

He would not even commit when asked if 30 weeks was too far into a pregnancy to destroy the child. In my mind that places him right up there with the former Democrat Virginia governor who said you could have the child born, set aside, and then discuss with the parents if they wanted to allow the child to live. Horrific!

I do realize abortion is a difficult political topic to navigate especially today and especially in the case of rape or incest. But whether a child is conceived in tragedy or conceived traditionally, the child created is still a child. Much like the Fetal Homicide Bill, if we admit a child is a child in one case, I'm not sure how we say it's not real in another.

Events involving those type of conceptions are sad, and they are tragic. I wish there were a middle path to take but there is not. Either a life will be taken, or someone will be forced to carry a child they do not want and will have a daily reminder of the horrific event that took place in their life. And if they chose to place the child up for adoption, they will have to deal with the mixed emotions of giving up the reminder while also surrendering someone that is a part of you and who you nurtured for nine months.

I've often said I want to save every child, but I also would be willing to work incrementally to save as many as I could along the way. An example I would use a lot is about a bus containing one hundred children that had crashed and was precariously hanging over a cliff, moments from going over and killing every child.

Based on how the bus was balancing, you figure quickly that you can save ninety-eight or ninety-nine children but there is no way to save all one hundred. If you try to save them all, you know the bus will go off the cliff and kill all one hundred. Faced with this dilemma, of course you would choose to save the ninety-eight or ninety-nine.

I would mourn the one or two children that had died. I would try to develop new technology to make sure all one hundred would be saved the next time. But I would not let all one hundred die because I could not save each and every one of them.

The Dobbs decision was historic. The overturning of Roe v. Wade was something I had hoped for, and something I had prayed for, for years. I know many of my colleagues were upset with the timing as I am sure it dampened what was supposed to be a red wave that year as it motivated the other side. However, for me, I celebrated the decision.

If I had my way, it would have occurred years earlier, and of course there was never going to be a good political year for it to occur. I think for so many years, politicians on both sides were able to use the issue as a way to gain support, never thinking it would change. I do imagine many like myself were sincere in their efforts, but I also believe some just knew it was a topic where you needed to pick the side the area supported in order to get elected.

Of course, the fight to protect life on all levels has not ended but getting it back to the states is a very good start. We must continue to fight to protect life and to educate individuals on the value of life.

CHAPTER THIRTY THREE

HE WHO IS WITHOUT SIN

When I first got to Frankfort as State Representative, there were at times we would deal with social conservative issues, from the Marriage Amendment, to adoptions, to the anti-bullying bill and others, several of which I hope to address in more detail throughout this book.

Many times, especially early on, I would get an email from someone usually in Danville and many times someone who would be from Centre College that would be more than critical especially when it came to issues dealing with certain communities that the Bible is clear that the action would be a sin.

Though extremely critical of my stances, it would always seem they were trying to influence me, sometimes with what they perceived as logic while others berating me. There were even a few times they tried to encourage me with some twisted interpretation of the Bible.

I always tried to address their concerns with what I hoped to be a Biblically based response and without demeaning their position. Many may not realize it, but I have always tried to avoid using the term "condemn." I always felt God did not delegate that power to me. We definitely have to speak the truth or as another friend said be fruit inspectors, but never condemn.

My response would be something to the effect of I appreciated your concerns. I would go onto to explain that hopefully I would handle the situation as Jesus handled the woman caught in adultery that they brought to him.

As you may recall from John 8, they brought a woman to Jesus who was caught in adultery and by their law she was to be stoned but they asked his opinion (really trying to trick him.) He first stooped down and wrote something on the ground with his finger and when he stood up, he said to them, "He that is without sin among you, let him first cast a stone at her."

He then bent down again and wrote on the ground more. Each of the accusers began to leave one at a time until they were all gone. When Jesus stood up and saw none but the woman left, he asked the woman where her accusers had gone and had no man condemned her.

She indicated no one. He then told her that He also did not condemn her. However, most people like to stop at this point. And certainly, if you were trying to make the argument that everything is ok, that there really is no sin, then this would be a good ending point.

However, He did go on and in his next line he said ". . . go, and sin no more." He didn't say go and rationalize your sin. He didn't say go and have your sin codified into the law. He said, "Go and sin no more."

Of course, many today confuse (or perhaps don't understand) what sin truly is. Some equate it to evil and, yes, to a certain degree that may be true. However, my understanding of sin is anything that begins the process of getting us farther and farther away from God.

Perhaps one of the bigger mistakes people of faith make is to equate different levels of sin. But when we do this, we begin to create separate categories so that we can more easily rationalize our sin or in our minds lessen the severity of our sin over some others.

Over the years this has led us to try to lessen the sin of sex before marriage, adultery, and so on. God knew we had these tendencies. Just look in Matthew 7:3-5 where He asked why are you worried about something small in your friend's eye when you have a beam in your eye? Take care of the beam in your own eye and then you can help your friend.

Jesus even went as far to say that if you look at a woman with lust in your heart who is not your wife you have already committed adultery. If you have anger in your heart towards your brother, then you have already committed murder.

So how is it that any of us can make it out of this world unscathed by the weapon of sin upon us? Well, you can't. What you can do is tap into the greatest gift God ever gave us, His son Jesus Christ.

If you make Jesus Christ your Lord and Savior, and ask for forgiveness of your sins, you have both forgiveness of your sins and eternal life after we pass from this world. Does that mean that you never sin again? Oh, if it were that easy.

Unfortunately, we still live in this world and are subject to the same temptations. What it does mean is we have this ultimate weight of sin removed from us and we know that our salvation is secure. God sends the Holy Spirit to guide us.

But for a second time, does this mean we never sin again? No, we can, and we will still fall but Jesus is there to pick us up. I think the best explanation I ever heard came from my wife, Lynn (or Peaches to our grandchildren.)

She said that yes you will still sin. You most definitely should make every effort not to, but at times you will fall. But, before salvation, Satan would use your sin to condemn you and make you think you are not worthy of God's Grace.

But after you have accepted Christ, He will use your sin to convict you. You will know what you have done is wrong, that it is a sin, and you will ask for forgiveness and work to get a little better every day. You will know that your salvation is secure.

But getting back to the topic, sadly, some people of faith as well as those pushing agendas that are tied to communities based on who they sleep with both have twisted God's word and His intentions I believe.

Some people in the LGBTQ+ communities have framed people of faith as hateful and have pushed not only to limit what they say but have gone as far as to have them jailed simply because they held a sincere believe in what is right and what is wrong according to the Bible.

On the other side, over the years, I have unfortunately heard some people of faith use language I will not repeat in this book to describe people in that community. I think it is important to remember that Jesus died for all of us including people in any community you might pick.

Set aside for a moment our discussion, early on I found it hard to understand how God's Grace was available say to someone who had brought harm to a child, but yes if they truly accept Christ as their Lord and confess their sins, then they too could find forgiveness.

Now that doesn't mean there are no earthly consequences, but they can find peace and freedom that their life after this world is secure. Back to the discussion at hand, I suppose my greatest concerns for some is that when someone becomes so comfortable in a sin and they have rationalized it for so long, that it may be difficult to lay all the sins on the alter because they believe their actions are not in fact a sin.

Perhaps my biggest concern is for certain faiths that in some ways are now condoning certain sins and, in some cases, celebrating. Once again, we have to take the log out of our own eye first, but I wouldn't want to stand before God after I passed and have to explain why I endorsed a sin when I was supposed to be leading a church.

We don't shut the doors to people. One of my former pastors said church is supposed to be a hospital for sinners and not a country club for saints. All are welcome through the doors. Where we have to draw the line is if someone is holding onto a sin, they cannot be in leadership, teach classes, etc. You can't let the patient run the clinic.

Jesus ate with sinners. He knew what they needed. And Jesus took flak from the "religious leaders of the time." But he did not become a sinner. He did not endorse their sins. He was there to free them from their sins and my hope for all is that you will find that freedom.

CHAPTER THIRTY FOUR

MARRIAGE AMENDMENT

During my first few years as State Representative, there was a big push throughout the country especially in the more conservative states to protect the traditional and Biblical definition of what a marriage was which was a uniting of one man and one woman. Obviously, in the more liberal states there was also a great deal of effort to redefine what a marriage was and to include same-sex unions in that definition.

The 2004 Legislative Session occurred during my second year of my first term as State Representative, so I was still a little green, but I was as I am now determined to do my best to follow the direction I believed God was leading me. Thankfully, there were also many like myself who had a fire in their belly to do what was right.

During that year, there were two major Marriage Amendments proposed. One was offered by the Republicans in the State Senate while the other one was surprisingly offered by a Democrat in the House. When further studying the one in the House it was realized this amendment had two issues rolled into the amendment which would allow it to seem as if Democrats were voting for traditional marriage but in reality, they knew that even if it passed the full process, a judge would probably throw it out before the citizens of Kentucky could vote on it since having two subjects in one amendment was not permitted by Kentucky's Constitution.

The Senate's version was passed and sent over to the House. The Democrat Majority Leadership in the House thought they would be crafty and so the Senate Version was passed out of the committee, but they were going to amend the bill to have it reflect the House version.

The House Republican Minority got together to discuss strategy and Governor Fletcher was included in some of the discussions. A decision was made that if the Democrats tried to amend the bill to include more than the one topic that we would walk out in protest. If we all walked out the Democrats could amend the bill but since it was a Constitutional Amendment, it would require a three-fifths vote or sixty members to pass the actual amended Amendment.

As it turned out, the Democrats did amend the bill to include two subjects and all the Republicans, and a small number of Democrats, walked out in protest. We proceeded to go to the front steps of the state capitol, where Governor Ernie Fletcher joined us. There were speeches by the Governor and Republican leadership.

After, some of us went to a side office to watch the continued debate. There were some Democrats on the floor cursing and angry that we had walked out. They said we were shirking our duty.

After the debate, a vote was taken, and the amended Amendment failed to pass because it lacked the sixty votes needed to leave the House. With no Republicans in the chamber and some of the more Liberal Democrats not wanting to be on record voting for traditional marriage even if it were a ruse, the Constitutional Amendment failed and the more Conservative Democrats would not have the political cover they had hoped for.

The following day, Democrat Leadership realized this might be disastrous for their more Conservative members. They had someone who had voted on the prevailing side make a motion to reconsider the bill. They then removed the amendment to the Amendment and allowed a floor vote on the original Senate bill. The bill did pass by a large margin and had a sufficient number to meet the 60-vote threshold. Even most Democrats voted for it except for the more Liberal ones.

Later that year, after a failed attempt to stop it in the courts, the Constitutional Amendment appeared on the ballot and passed with around 75% of Kentuckians voting in favor of the Amendment. As you may know, the US Supreme Court nullified the validity of the Amendment just a few years later. The Amendment remains in our Kentucky Constitution but has no effect until if and when the US Supreme Court reverses.

CHAPTER THIRTY FIVE

BULLIED BY A BILL

Early on in my legislative career there was a bill that kept resurfacing for several years. It was known as, "The Bullying Bill." It was sold on the idea that kids obviously should not be bullied. And on that I agreed.

Now I have a distinct understanding of what it means to be bullied. The doctor once noted on my charts that I was overweight and pigeon-toed. I also made good grades. Being overweight, pigeon-toed, and making good grades, you can only imagine how very much I understood bullying both verbally and physically.

Now thankfully during my time, physical bullying usually meant getting beat up and not someone trying to take your life. Thankfully, I had a father that told me the same thing I told my kids, "I don't want to hear about you starting a fight, but if someone starts one with you, I want to hear that you finished it."

Usually, my encounters would probably be best described as what people used to call "boys fighting." I'm not even sure I told my parents half the time. I remember once my older brother and I were walking to our church across from the school in Burgin for Christmas play practice. I was always a shepherd, but I think my older brother might have been Joseph that year.

As we walked over, one of the older boys that was at our school decided he needed to "teach me a lesson," or get out his frustrations or something. My older brother just kept going. Maybe because he didn't want to be late or maybe because he knew I could handle myself even though I would and did lose.

After the fight, I headed onto the church for practice as well. The one thing I learned early in life is you have to stand up to bullies. You're probably going to lose more than you win, but you can fight them now or fight every day later.

I also remember a time after we moved to Boyle County, when I was riding the bus. I got on the bus and took a front seat, but a much older, and apparently meaner, student got on the bus and told me I and the other student had to move. When I was not quick enough to get up, he punched me as hard as he could in the arm.

In addition, while at school, he would come up to me and punch me in the arm and walk off. He also had a friend that hung out with him. Now some might call his friend a "toadie" like in "A Christmas Story," but he was much taller than the bully. Some might say his friend was more intimidating than him, but other than just being there he was quiet and did not engage with the bully in fights.

Now I knew I was going to have to stand up to this bully so when I got on the bus, I went to the front seat and sat down. When the bully came up, he started beating on me for a small bit until the bus driver got on and since he was bigger than the bully, he took care of it.

Getting back to the "Bullying Bill," I had an understanding what it meant to be bullied. However, if you looked closely at the bill, especially some of the earlier versions, you could see it was merely an attempt to create a backdoor indoctrination of our children into "alternative lifestyles."

If people choose to live their life a certain way, I may have spiritual concerns for them, but it is their life. What is not their life is our children and they should have no right to indoctrinate our children.

So, being in the minority, I knew my ability to stop or slow this bill was limited. What I ended up doing is creating an amendment I placed on the bill so that if they brought up the bill, I could force them to take a vote on my amendment.

The amendment to the bill read something to this effect, "Nothing in this bill shall be misconstrued to require someone to teach or to be taught something that is in direct contradiction to their personal religious beliefs." I considered this a very First Amendment friendly amendment. If the goal was to keep kids safe and not indoctrinate them, then this amendment did nothing to prevent that.

However, if the goal were to normalize an "alternative lifestyle" then my amendment certainly minimized or derailed that effort. Democrats in leadership were furious. They knew if they called up, "The Bullying Bill," I would call my amendment and not only would the Republicans in the minority support the amendment, but there would also be plenty of conservative Democrats who would vote for as well and the amendment would probably pass.

What Democrats did instead was to sit on the bill and not call it up. This made several of the special interest groups like the "Fairness Alliance," extremely mad at me and they worked at every angle. I even had a priest pull me out of the debate briefly to try and convince me to pull the amendment or at least not call it. It was the first and only time I recall a priest actually cursing me out.

After his expressed concerns, I got back on the floor quickly as I was afraid that they would try to quickly call the bill up while I had stepped out of the chamber. In the defense of the priest, I don't think he fully understood what the bill truly did but I was bit surprised at his method of trying to convince me.

Over the years, they tried different versions of that bill and they did eventually pass a "Bullying Bill" that removed most of the more aggreges text, but it took several years of me standing up to them before their success.

At times I would even receive threating calls and emails, one even from Germany for some reason. One time I got a request to interview from Anderson Cooper regarding my stance. The timing of his request made it difficult for me to do the interview.

He had wanted to do my interview in a 24-hour window and that was too tight for me. Also, I had called my pastor to run it by him and he said they just wanted to make me look bad. And he was right. I couldn't make the interview work, but they used a clip from one I did with WHAS 11 news. Though he tried with the clip, he wasn't very successful in making me look bad, but he had interviewed others that had a similar position to myself who he did in fact frame in a poor manner.

I remember one year, The Fairness Alliance representative tried to trick me. He said he surrendered and agreed to the text I had wanted. He even brought me a copy of the amendment that he had a supportive legislator have a bill drafter draft.

After he left, I thoroughly reviewed the amendment, but something was wrong that I just couldn't place my finger on. It was true that the text I wanted was in the amendment, but it wasn't underlined. When amending an existing statute, I knew new language is underlined and I knew this was new language.

I called a bill drafter and I asked, "What's up with this?" He indicated that yes, if passed, this text would be part of the law, but it would not be codified so it would not make it into the statutes. The only ones that would know it was law would be those of us who had passed it.

I would love to say that was the only time The Fairness Alliance had tried to trick me, but it was not. Over the years, I had always had an open-door policy. It didn't matter if we agreed on an issue or not. I would be happy to meet with you.

Now The Fairness Alliance lobbyist was always trying to change my mind on this and other bills. I even remember one time he asked me for a hug. I think he might have been a bit surprised when I in fact hugged him. But I had no hate in my heart for him. I just wanted to protect my and Kentucky's kids.

On one particular time, my Legislative Assistant let me know that The Fairness Alliance lobbyist had two of my Boyle County constituents up front that wanted to visit with me. As I always did if I had time, I said, "Sure, have them come on back."

Now, there were two of my constituents with him. However, what he hadn't told my Legislative Assistant was that there were also about another ten individuals and when they came into my office, they surrounded my desk and tried to intimidate me to be supportive of their issues. I did take the time to listen and when they left, I changed my policy on visiting with anyone.

I no longer would visit with The Fairness Alliance in my office. I did this not because I disagreed with what they were pushing (even though I did) but because their representative had lied and misrepresented something to me. I will tolerate a lot, but not lying to me.

CHAPTER THIRTY SIX

———————

OH HOW WE HAVE DILUTED THE WORD "RACIST"

My first couple of years as a Legislator started out a little rocky or perhaps you would say I faced many challenges. After figuring out where the bathrooms were in Frankfort, we faced battles on "The Fetal Homicide Bill," "The Marriage Amendment," and "Pension Bills," but perhaps the most controversial bill I spoke on was "The Cloning Bill."

There was a push early in my career to ban cloning and I believe this was something we needed to do. However, there were many others, including some in Republican Leadership at the time that wanted to put the exception of "Therapeutic Cloning" into the bill.

For those who haven't followed, Therapeutic Cloning involves creating a clone of a human, growing that clone for a period of time, and then destroying the clone to harvest the stem cells. So, you create life and then destroy life all in the name of science. As you can imagine, I was horrified people could even conceive of doing this especially since adult stem cells which do not require the destruction of life had been found to have been so much more effective at that time.

Before the House was about to vote on the bill as well as possibly an amendment to the bill which would include the exception, the Republican House Caucus gathered to discuss. Now the universities very much wanted the exception and one of our members who I believe was sincere said the universities had said a cloned human was not a life.

Most people see me as calm, but on issues I'm passionate about I used to get worked up pretty quickly. When the member said the universities indicated it wasn't a life, I responded something to the effect of, "Well, they're wrong and they are lying." Leadership called on me to settle down, but I said I would not.

I indicated it is very clear to me and anyone who stopped to review that a cloned human in fact was a life and a human and it was appalling to think someone would be so callous with life.

When we went to the floor of the House and the bill was called up, the debate was fierce. When it was my time to speak, I spoke of how the idea of cloning a human only to destroy the child for science was evil. I even compared it to the evils of slavery on multiple levels.

Unfortunately, that did not set well with one of our members, Paul Bather. When it was his time to speak, he did not debate the merits of the bill but instead verbally attacked me. He said as white man, I did not have the right to compare anything to slavery and that I was a racist for doing so.

Now, as you can imagine, being still relatively new to the KY General Assembly, this was a tough punch. I had merely called slavery evil (which it was) and had made a comparison to cloning which I thought was evil. Many of my colleagues called on me to call for a point of privilege to dispute the personal attack and maybe I should have, but I was a bit in shock with the accusation.

Thankfully, there were others that stood up in my defense and oddly enough one of them happened to be a fellow freshman colleague of mine. Derrick Graham and I had come into the House in the same class, but he was a Democrat. He also is an African American.

When it was Representative Graham's turn, he stood up and calmly said that although he disagreed with my comparison and my position on the bill, he did not consider me to be a racist. That kind gesture has stayed with me since then and I will forever be grateful to my colleague and someone I consider to be a friend.

Yes, we are generally on opposite sides politically, but I am thankful that at that time you could have friends on both sides of the aisle despite the debates on the floor. After the Session had ended and I was preparing to head out for the day, I had several other African American Democrats approach me and apologize for Representative Bather. They indicated that was just Paul. I explained I appreciated them coming to me. But it was important for them to know I cared about everyone, and it was unfortunate someone tried to label me something I was not.

I will say that event helped me establish a good relationship with legislators on the other side of the aisle. I could have chosen to be bitter, but after the initial impact, I grew even more to care about others regardless of whether they agreed with me or not and whether they looked like me or not. I will always cherish those relationships.

CHAPTER THIRTY SEVEN

IT'D BE OK IF YOU WON, BUT...

During my first race for Auditor in 2015, there wasn't the same amount of focus on my race as there was for the Attorney General. True, I had raised only $45,000 while my opponent had raised over $800,000, but so many more people were concerned about the AG's race.

I suppose the main reason most people focused on that race was because when Ernie Fletcher got elected in 2003, he was the first Republican governor Kentucky had seen since the 1960's when Louie Nunn got elected. Unfortunately, Greg Stumbo, a Democrat, had also got elected to Kentucky's Attorney General position.

Since I had served with Representative/Majority Floor Leader Stumbo in the House, I knew a little bit about his actions. I even commented when he was elected that he would probably be a thorn in Ernie Fletcher's side.

It was not too long after they both took office that AG Stumbo worked on trying to take down Governor Fletcher and that he did. The Merit scandal became a wound the Governor could not survive.

Granted, some of the fault was in fact due to Fletcher's staff and his response to the incident. What he was hit with was nothing the Democrat's hadn't done for years, but they were simply better at not leaving an easy trail to follow.

Still, Fletcher had campaigned on cleaning up Frankfort, and though his heart was in the right place, his inability to constrain staff and supporters who had waited a generation to be on top resulted in a wound he did not recover from. Fletcher remained in office, but his reelection efforts fail short, and we were once again faced with another eight years of Democrat rule in the governor's office.

With that in mind, as Matt Bevin campaigned for governor, he knew the importance of getting a Republican Attorney General, not to cover things up, but to be a partner who worked to clean up government instead of trying to lay traps for a future opponent. Our candidate for AG in the fall was Whitney Westerfield.

Whitney was (and is) a good man, but he was facing Andy Beshear, the Governor at the time, Steve Beshear's son, so the money flowed in large amounts to Andy's coffers. They found every little thing they could to hit Whitney with.

Whitney did end up having some funds to campaign with (much more than me,) but he also had faced a Primary previously which he had to use a good portion of his war chest. Oddly enough, his opponent in the Primary, Michael Hogan, years later was prosecuted and convicted by the FBI after my office as Auditor did a referral of an audit we did on his County Attorney office.

Whitney also received support from a couple of superPACs that tried to balance things out. That race was very tight in all the polling.

With all that in mind, the last day before the election, Matt Bevin, who was running for governor, chartered a plane and wanted our entire slate to travel with him. As we traveled the state, we had a good chance to visit. When we stopped to get something to eat, Matt looked at me and said, "Mike, I'd love to have you, but I got to have Whitney."

Now I got what the future Governor Bevin was saying, and he probably was correct as Whitney barely lost to Andy Beshear who ended up being a thorn in Bevin's side and eventually beat Bevin when he ran for reelection. But couldn't Bevin had just said, "Mike, I need you and Whitney to win."

But that was Bevin. He was a good governor, but unfortunately, he was his worst enemy. I know during the 2019 race in which he lost, and I won reelection to Auditor, he made a comment on camera that night that made both my daughters mad and they really wanted to go tell him so.

When I did my victory speech, I told the same joke I had told during that year. In addition to thanking everyone, I said, "Well, I'm glad I won reelection. I was trying to think of what I would do if I lost. I thought, well, maybe I could start a company cleaning mirrors? I'm not sure why. It's just something I could see myself doing."

Bevin, when he was giving his speech, he talked about how great everyone else did, but when he got to me, he just said, "I'm not sure why Mike told that joke. I told him on the bus it wasn't any good." I suppose since it was evident he wasn't going to win, and he needed someone to vent on. I guess I was as good as any since I, as all the other Republicans, had won.

My daughters were angry, but I knew how Bevin was and sadly I knew even before the election he was not going to get reelected. I guess if he needed a punching bag, so be it. I was blessed with a second term, and he was headed home.

Another little-known fact during that time was I inadvertently gave President Trump half his quote he used to describe Governor Bevin the day after the election. While Trump was in for a rally to try and help Bevin and the rest of the slate he asked me, "Do you think Bevin can win?"

Having travelled the state, I knew the odds were not in Bevin's favor. I simply commented, "Well, it's going to be close, but hopefully you can drag him across the finish line."

As you may or may not remember, the day after the election after all other Republicans had won except Bevin, President Trump tweeted something to the effect, "Bevin was down 10-15 points but I almost drug him across the finish line."

At least my encounter with President Trump did get me a signed red hat that stated, "KEEP AUDITING GREAT, MikeHarmon.com."

**2019 Election Night
Auditor. Mike Harmon Speech**
https://www.facebook.com/share/v/
nuNM5wv1wrquirJW/?mibextid=ox5AEW

2019 Election Photo L-R Tori, Mah, Aiden, Mike (PaPaw), Lynn (Peaches), HaMoody, Lizzie

On the trail during my 2019 reelection at the Monroe County Parade

On the trail during my 2019 reelection.
L-R Mike (PaPaw), Congressman Andy Barr

159

On the trail during my 2019 reelection.

On the trail during my 2019 reelection. L-R Mike (PaPaw), Mike Duncan

On the trail during my 2019 reelection. L-R Nick Nash, Mike (PaPaw)

ABOVE:
On the trail during my
2019 reelection.
PreDebate Supporters.

LEFT:
On the trail during my
2019 reelection.
L-R Congressman James
Comer, Mike (PaPaw)

On the trail during my 2019 reelection. L-R Mike (PaPaw), Robert Stivers, Ralph Alvarado,
Allison Ball, Michael Adams, Ryan Quarles, Daniel Cameron

CHAPTER THIRTY EIGHT

FOLLOW THE DATA

When I was campaigning for my first term as Auditor, much of what I presented was very data driven. I travelled around the state and spoke about my concerns including the states pension systems.

One of the things that I did while in the House was to make sure that I worked hard for everyone regardless of their political persuasions. Sure, if there was an issue that I was passionate about, I would fight hard for that issue. But if someone needed something or needed to access some existing help,

I didn't check their party before trying to help them navigate the process, I just asked, "What do you need?"

When I got into the Auditor's office, and I addressed staff on that first day, I told everyone I don't want to hear you are targeting anyone or giving anyone a pass, I just want you to follow the data.

My Comms Director, Michael Goins, heard those words and decided that we would coin the phrase, "Follow The Data." And that is what we did. The phase became a motto that in very simple terms described the direction I wanted to see the office pursue.

The Executive Staff even went as far as to suggest that we should develop a "Follow The Data" pin and logo. There were a few suggestions made and even though I had suggested using a spotlight on the logo, I went ahead and agreed to the design that used a magnifying glass.

That was the design most of the executive staff had voted for and in this case, I accepted their guidance. We (myself and the executive staff) also all chipped in so that no taxpayer dollars would be spent on the pins.

In addition to wearing them ourselves, we also shared with the rest of the staff and friends. Anytime someone started new, we would give them a pin and thankfully our stock lasted until I finished my last term.

One additional funny aspect of the motto was that the first couple of years at the Auditor's office we would hold a Halloween party as a fundraiser for the KECC fundraising drive. During one of those events, I dressed as the "Star Trek Next Generation," character, "Data." Somewhere during the day, it was suggested that I have some of the other individuals in costume follow me and take a picture of the group. That way we could say everyone was following the "Data."

I truly appreciated the eight years that the citizens of Kentucky entrusted me with as Auditor, and I hope that we were successful in carrying out our motto of "Following The Data."

CHAPTER THIRTY NINE

PEACHES PERFECT

God has truly blessed me over the years. I am blessed with a wonderful wife, Lynn. We have, as of July 2024, been married for over 34 years. Of course, our marriage, like anyone else's, has not been perfect, but we have been faithful to each other, and our love has only continued to grow. I believe our secret to success can best be described as we have both worked to put God first, and our marriage and family second.

Although we knew each other growing up as we attended the same church, Lynn is a few years older than I am (though she looks a lot younger.) So, while attending church as youths, I'm not sure she ever even noticed me, but I certainly noticed her.

As it turned out, we went our separate ways and so for the years after I went to college, I did not see her. I would love to say I thought of her often while at college but as you remember, she probably barely knew my name while we were at church, so I did not.

As I was getting closer to finishing college, a mutual friend of ours was getting married and getting married at the church we grew up in. I had come home from college that weekend and though invited to the wedding, I was so tired, I did not plan to attend.

But something happened and I made a last-minute decision to go to the wedding. Both my parents had worked at American Greetings at times, so we had a lot of extra cards at the house. I grabbed a card that seemed somewhat appropriate, shoved a $10 bill into it, and headed to the church.

As it turned out, it was a good wedding, and I enjoyed visiting with some of my old friends. There was also one beautiful red head (Lynn) I noticed there, but I assumed she was out of my league (because she was.) I did speak to her briefly. Several of our friends were having an after-wedding reception get-together and I was invited. Thankfully, Lynn was also invited. At the gathering, a few people were playing a game that used both cards and spoons and Lynn and I both were in the game. During the day Lynn and I got to talking and she indicated she was struggling with a college Math class and wanted to know if I would be willing to tutor her. Of course I agreed.

I called her later (barely able to get my nerve up to call her) and we agreed on a time to get together. Although the ruse was a tutoring session, it was apparently to my excitement a date. That first date was on a Friday the 13th and since that time we try to celebrate Friday the 13th regardless of what month they might fall.

To make a long story short, we did start dating and I eventually asked her to marry me. The interesting thing was the friend who I had almost not gone to his wedding ended up being the pastor who performed our wedding ceremony. I have been blessed ever since.

We are also blessed with two children, Tori and Lizzie (Butterbean,) as well as a wonderful son-in-law who we call, Mah. He is from Syria and Tori and him met in Ghana Africa.

Tori and Mah have two children, Aiden and HaMoody. These two wonderful grandchildren made Lynn and I, Peaches and PaPaw and we will be forever grateful for God's blessings of these two.

The family at Stanford Drive-In.
L-R Mike (PaPaw), Aiden, Lynn (Peaches), Mah, Tori, HaMoody

L-R Congressman Dan Crenshaw,
Mike (PaPaw), Lynn (Peaches)

Mike & Lynn's
Wedding Photo

L-R Lynn (Peaches), Sarah Huckabee Sanders, Mike (PaPaw)

L-R Lynn, Mike at a Boyle County GOP event

CHAPTER FORTY

AUDITORS DON'T MAKE
A LOT OF FRIENDS

I used to get asked if the people we audited would get mad. Thankfully, most of the people we audited would have a clean audit and then the only thing that might upset them would be the bill from the audit.

One of my auditors said her Dad always told her there were two lies told at an entrance conference to an audit. The first was from the auditor when they said, "We are just here to help," and the other was the auditee who replied, "Well, I'm glad you're here."

Now I'm not sure the joke is 100% accurate as I do believe we wanted to help an agency be the best they could be but certainly it makes for a good joke.

Auditing was interesting. Most people were audited by us because the law required my office to audit them. As I said, most of them were fine with our work other than maybe the bill primarily because most people tried to do a good job and by extension most audits had little if any findings.

Perhaps the people who would be most angry at us would be the ones we decided ourselves they needed to be audited or perhaps we were called upon to audit and agreed it was necessary to audit them. Inevitably, there were generally always some findings with these types of audits. So, yes, in these cases, we did not make a lot of friends.

The line I used was, "Well, I had a coach once say if you want a friend, get a dog. So, I got a dog." But as I said, most people respected and appreciated what the office did, so we were good.

However, when I decided to seek higher office, it did make fundraising challenging as even if someone liked you, if they were an official you had to be careful about asking for support for fear it might create a perceived or even actual conflict.

In addition, once I announced my race for governor, I had to directly recuse myself from any audits that intersected with the governor's office. In auditing terms, we would consider that an impairment and we put up additional firewalls to protect the auditee, our auditors, and myself.

I could certainly still speak about any audit my office completed (as anyone in the public could) but I could not be part of any of the processes or reviews until completed.

In addition, although a state auditor usually has a strong grasp of how government works, they have a harder time moving up to higher office because, "Auditor's don't make a lot of friends."

CHAPTER FORTY ONE

FIRST GRANDCHILD

First children are great, but first grandchildren are even better. I have two grandsons at the writing of this book, and I love them both so very much. But when you have that first grandchild, you just view the world a little differently.

Our first grandchild made me a PaPaw and my wife a Peaches. Of course, this was during a great turmoil in our life. My oldest daughter and mother of our grandchildren had to leave her husband (who was from Syria) in Ghana, Africa when she was seven months pregnant while we tried to figure out how to get him to the states. She gave birth to our first grandchild, Aiden, but had to wait almost 2 years before she could hold her husband again and he could hold his son.

While we prayed for the day my son-in-law would be able to reunite with his wife, my wife and I still made sure our new grandson got as much love as possible. Some of the faces he made were so hilarious while others were so cute.

I do have to admit that I did do one posting to social media with Aiden with this perfect face and the caption something to the effect of, "You do want to vote for my PaPaw for Auditor, don't you?"

As I said, there was a lot of turmoil that year. Our eldest trying to get her husband home and our youngest in an abusive relationship was a challenge. As well as all the accidents I had during that campaign. It is a wonder we survived and even more a miracle that I won my race.

However, it was good that I won my race. With our level of income, I'm not sure we could have scraped together the close to $20,000 it took to keep our son-n-law alive in Ghana and get him home to unite with his family. We also may have never been blessed with our second grandson, HaMoody.

But God is good, and PaPaw and Peaches are so happy to have been blessed with two wonderful grandsons. As for HaMoody, he had his moment in the sun when on my 2019 election night Barstool Sports took a clip of what appeared to be him punching out my daughter while she held him. She was of course fine, but the clip received over 1.5 thousand repost and fifteen thousand likes.

Post to Bar Stool Sports of clip of what appeared to be Hamoody slugging his Mother on Election Night 2019

https://x.com/barstoolstweets/status/
1191906011768119297?s=46

As I said, grandchildren change your life, and they change your point of view. My eldest grandson loves roll playing and reenacts things he has seen on YouTube. During this play, as he switches back and forth from different characters, he states the character's name and then says POV.

At first, I wasn't sure what he was doing, and then I realized he was indicating he was performing from their point of view. That is one of the main reasons I finally settled on the title of "PaPaw's POV".

I have had a lot of different points of view over the years, child, son, husband, father, grandfather, candidate, and so on. Hopefully, I have done my best to weave my faith into all of those and put God first. And I have appreciated and loved all those roles, but being a PaPaw is just something different. I will forever be grateful to God for that particular POV.

PaPaw and HaMoody (18 days old) L-R Mike (PaPaw), HaMoody

PaPaw and the boys. L-R Mike (PaPaw), HaMoody, Aiden

Family at Shakertown L-R Lizzie, Lynn (Peaches), Aiden, HaMoody, Mike (PaPaw)

PaPaw and HaMoody relaxing with a snack. L-R Mike (PaPaw), HaMoody

L-R HaMoody, Lynn (Peaches), Aiden having a meal at Zaxby's (Jan 2024)

Grandparents Day L-R HaMoody, Mike (PaPaw), Lynn (Peaches)

Grandparents Day L-R Mike (PaPaw), Aiden, Lynn (Peaches)

PaPaw's first grandchild.
(July 04, 2015) L-R Aiden, Mike (PaPaw)

That time PaPaw and Peaches got #2.
Son in Law Mah with new son
L-R Mahmoud, HaMoody (Silas)

When Lynn became Peaches.
L-R Lynn(Peaches), Aiden

You do want to vote for my
PaPaw for Auditor, don't you?

L-R MaMaw Janet (Mike's Mom), Aiden, Mike (PaPaw)

That time I Mc'd an event at a ballpark and someone should have told me to compensate for the echo. L-R Mike (PaPaw), Daniel Di Martino, Congressman Andy Barr

Top L-R Darrell (Mike's Dad), Janet (Mike's Mom/ MaMaw Janet),
Bottom L-R Darrell (Mike's Dad/PaPaw Harmon), Lizzie

L-R Scott Jennings, Mike (PaPaw)

Spectrum News In Focus L-R Mario Anderson, Mike (PaPaw)

WYMT Issues & Answers L-R Steve Hensley, Mike (PaPaw)

Auditor Mike Harmon Official Photo

Committee Testimony L-R ASA Farrah Petter, Mike (PaPaw), COS Jon Grate

KECC Halloween Fundraiser "Follow The Data (Star Trek)"
L-R Mike (PaPaw), Michael Goins, Alta Renfro, Sara Beth Gregory

Last Day Mike was physically at the Auditor Office after cleaning out office

Reviewing legislation on the floor of the Kentucky House of Representatives
L-R Mike, Rep. Joe Fischer

L-R Mike (PaPaw), Comms Director Michael Goins

L-R Mike (PaPaw), Sen. (former Rep.)
CB Embry

L-R Mike (PaPaw), Jason Chaffetz

Mike Maggard's Barn

L-R Mike (PaPaw), Daughter Lizzie on the trail in 2015

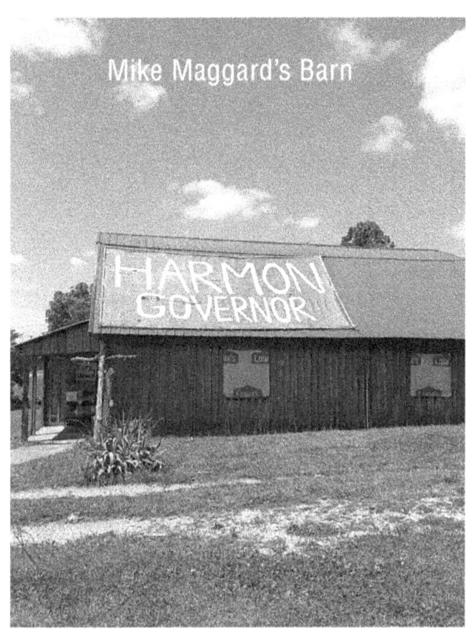

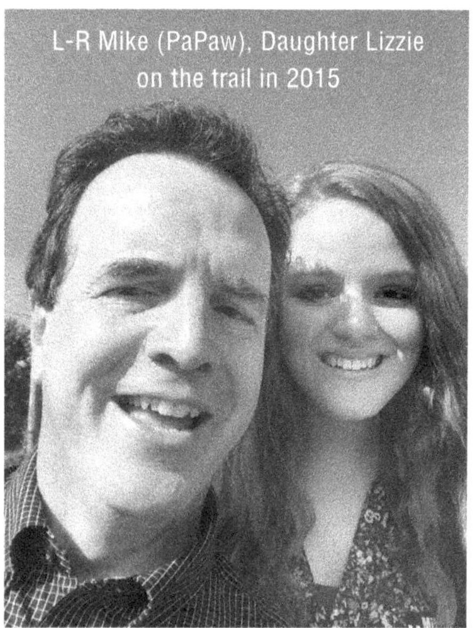

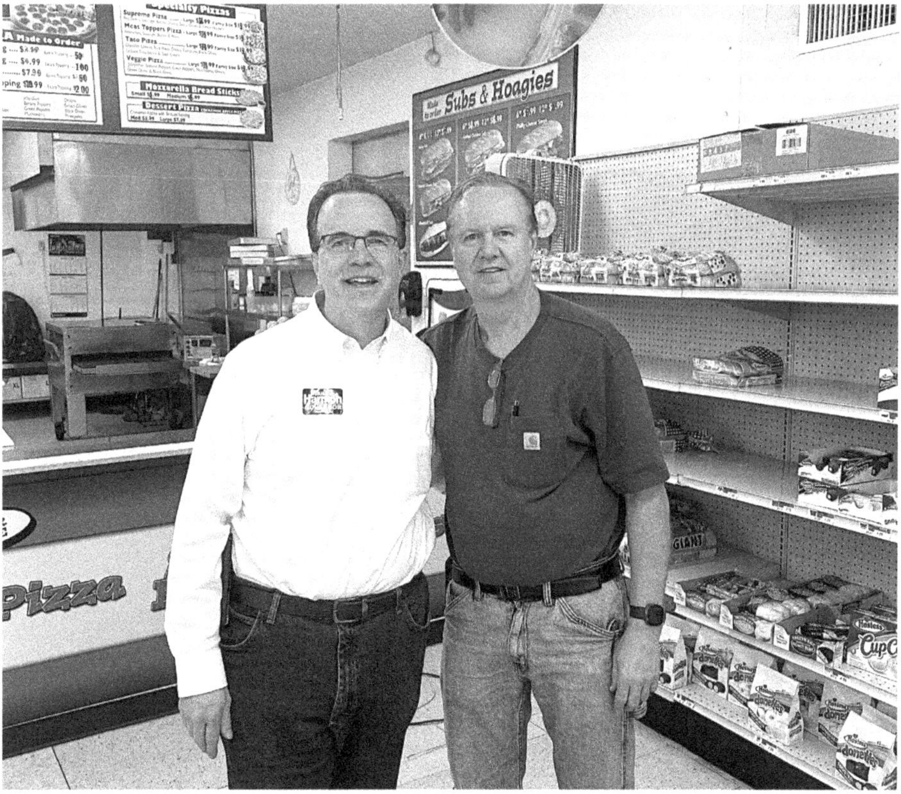

L-R Mike (PaPaw), Former State Representative Tim Couch at his store.

L-R Mike (PaPaw), Jon Grate, Daniel McQuerry

L-R Mike, Senator Jim Bunning